JOHANN KILIAN, PASTOR

A Wendish Lutheran
in Germany and Texas

By

George R. Nielsen

Texas Wendish Heritage Society

Serbin, Texas

ISBN: 1-4033-7989-0 (e-book)
ISBN: 1-4033-7990-4 (Paperback)
ISBN: 1-4033-7991-2 (Hardcover)

Library of Congress Control Number: 2002094950

This book is printed on acid free paper.

Printed in the United States of America
Bloomington, IN

1stBooks – rev. 08/28/03

To the memory of my father

William H. Nielsen (1901 - 2001)

who had the good sense to marry a Wendish knježna.

Contents

Illustrations

PREFACE

There is no indication that Johann Kilian ever considered his life sufficiently significant and worthy of a biography. Would that he had anticipated it and had showered his biographer with boxes of sources and diaries full of his secret thoughts. He did not; yet the life he led, with the way he led it, lends itself to such a study.

Kilian lived in a dramatically changing environment. The western world was entering the industrial age, and he departed the country of his birth on a newly constructed railroad. Europe was on the move, and he was part of the massive migration flooding out of Europe into many parts of the world. The intellectual movements of nationalism and ethnic awareness were part of his experience. That was the first part of his life. Then he settled in a part of Texas, not quite on the frontier itself, but in an isolated area of a post oak forest. There his life, to a large extent, was pre-industrial, his travel was restricted by a primitive transportation system, and his intellectual life was undernourished from an absence of colleagues and stimulating literature. Within this context of both progressive and retrogressive change, Kilian demonstrated a vast capacity for adaptability.

Yet within his religious framework Kilian was anything but adaptable. There he maintained a continuity and a consistency. His gyroscope in life was a faith based on Scripture, Luther, and the Confessions; and that faith he found difficult to compromise. As a result, Kilian's fixed beliefs were constantly challenged by the changing context of society. His response to each setting provides the dynamism of this study.

Kilian's life should be instructive for a variety of readers. It provides information on the Wends, a Slavic ethnic group. It expands the history of immigration to Texas and the settlement of an area of the state. And it looks into the religious life of people and the issues that were important to them. But most of all, it is the biography of a person, revealing how he holds fast to certain principles, and applies them in an environment of change.

The major hurdle that confronted me in writing Kilian's biography was the collection, transcription, and translation of his letters. Kilian adopted a practice of first writing a draft of a letter which he then revised with insertions and deletions. After making the copy to be mailed, he filed the draft for future reference. Very few of his revised letters have been found, but more than two hundred of his drafts remain. A large number were kept with the records of the Serbin congregation and eventually the congregation placed them with the Concordia Historical Institute at St. Louis for safekeeping. A second portion was at one time in the possession of Hermann Schmidt, the pastor who succeeded Hermann Kilian in Serbin. These letters were placed in the Texas Wendish Heritage Society Archives in Serbin by his daughter's family and were listed under the Blasig Collection. Many drafts and revised letters are also in the congregational archives of *Trinitatisgemeinde* at Weigersdorf. Some of the letters that were mailed are found in the Sorbian Institute (*Serbski Institut*) at Bautzen or were printed in the Wendish newspaper of that time.

While Kilian's use of Wendish and German was that of an educated person and his handwriting was relatively legible, his use of the old German script and his insertions and changes made reading more difficult. Several people have been indispensable in assisting me in making these drafts usable as historical sources. Dr. Siegmund Musiat of the Sorbian Institute in Bautzen translated the letters written in Wendish into German. Gertrude Mahling, (Trudla Malinkowa) Wendish historian and editor of *Pomhaj Bóh*, not only helped me in locating letters but also provided me with guidance and read the draft of the chapter on Europe. Bill E. Biar, a lifelong friend, now of Carrollton, Texas, has transcribed and translated the majority of the letters and corrected many more. And finally I must acknowledge my father, William Nielsen, who worked with many of the letters and who also tutored me in the German script and language.

In addition I would like to extend my gratitude to Dr. Dietrich Scholze of the *Serbski Institut* in Bautzen for support and assistance. For assistance in research I must acknowledge the work of Barbara Hilscher of the Texas Wendish Society Museum in Serbin, The Rev. Mark A. Loest of Concordia Historical Institute, and Pastor Michael Voigt of *Trinitatisgemeinde* in Weigersdorf. Harold Smith, of Winner, South Dakota, graciously read the manuscript and pointed out numerous flaws. And finally, I thank Dr. Joseph Wilson for making his extensive research on the *Ben Nevis* passengers available to me.

Johann Kilian, Pastor

Johann Kilian 1876
Source: Texas Wendish Heritage Society

1
KILIAN IN EUROPE 1811-1854

As Johann Kilian, the young pastor of the small Saxon village of Kotitz, closed the door of the parsonage on St. Michael's Day in 1848, he knew he had closed the door on a life that he had found most satisfying and secure. His decision to leave was not a sudden detached decision, but a logical step resulting from a small step he had taken months earlier. Little had he known that the small initial step would eventually lead to his departure from the Kotitz parish. But this new step to a new parish also would have consequences. And it would be followed by other logical steps that would lead to a life he could never have imagined.

He had been the pastor in Kotitz for eleven years, since 1837, when he was installed as the successor of his deceased uncle, Michael Kilian. Kotitz had been an ideal parish for him. It was a familiar community, not far from his childhood home. The parish was small enough so that he could engage in all aspects of the ministry, including creative pursuits, as well as the daily routines expected of a parish pastor. He was financially secure as a pastor in the Saxon state church and his home with the garden and fruit trees provided peace and serenity. But he was also young and energetic. The call to the new parish, with all of its insecurity, did provide him with a cause that he believed in and that it was worth leaving all these pleasant conditions behind.[1]

The young pastor had been born on March 22, 1811, into a Europe filled with turmoil. Europe in 1811 was a scene of intense nationalism, a movement spawned by the French Revolution of 1789. Feudalism, which had focused on a small geographical areas, gave way to large nations with centralized administrations and bureaucracies. People began viewing themselves as citizens of a nation rather than only as residents of a locality, and, instead of giving their loyalty to a lord, they gave it to the nation-state. As the rulers attempted to expand the size and power of their nations, they developed large armies and engaged in wars against other nations. Not since the religious wars of 1618 - 1648 had there been so much unrest in central Europe.

Countries allied themselves with other countries, alliances fought each other, peace treaties were written, and diplomats drew and redrew national boundaries. By 1811 France, led by Napoleon, had gained control of most of continental Europe and was preparing to invade Russia. There was no unified Germany and the numerous German states could not agree on foreign policy and on which nations should be their allies or enemies. Prussia, an emerging German state, opposed Napoleon while Kilian's homeland of Saxony allied itself with him. When Johann was only two, the war came close to home and just a few miles away at the village of Hochkirch, where his grandparents lived, Napoleon defeated an army of Russians and Prussians. But Napoleon eventually lost the war, and Saxony paid the price for choosing Napoleon by being stripped of almost half of its territory. The victors, meeting at Vienna, took away all of Lower Lusatia, as well as that part of Upper Lusatia which years earlier had belonged to Silesia, and ceded it to Prussia. Saxony retained the remaining part of Upper Lusatia, where the Kilian family lived.

Though Prussia and Saxony were then political units with changing boundaries, Lusatia is a geographical area in eastern Germany. On the south are the mountains separating it from The Czech Republic, and on the east is the Oder River, the boundary line with Poland. The Spree River flows northward from the mountains through the chief towns of Bautzen and Cottbus, on through a swampy area called the Spreewald, and then through Berlin. The southern part, because it was higher in altitude is called Upper Lusatia while the northern part is named Lower Lusatia.

The people who originally occupied Lusatia were Slavic, called "Wends" by the Germans, or "Sorbs," a term used in contemporary times. Johann Kilian came from this Slavic heritage.[2] In earlier times

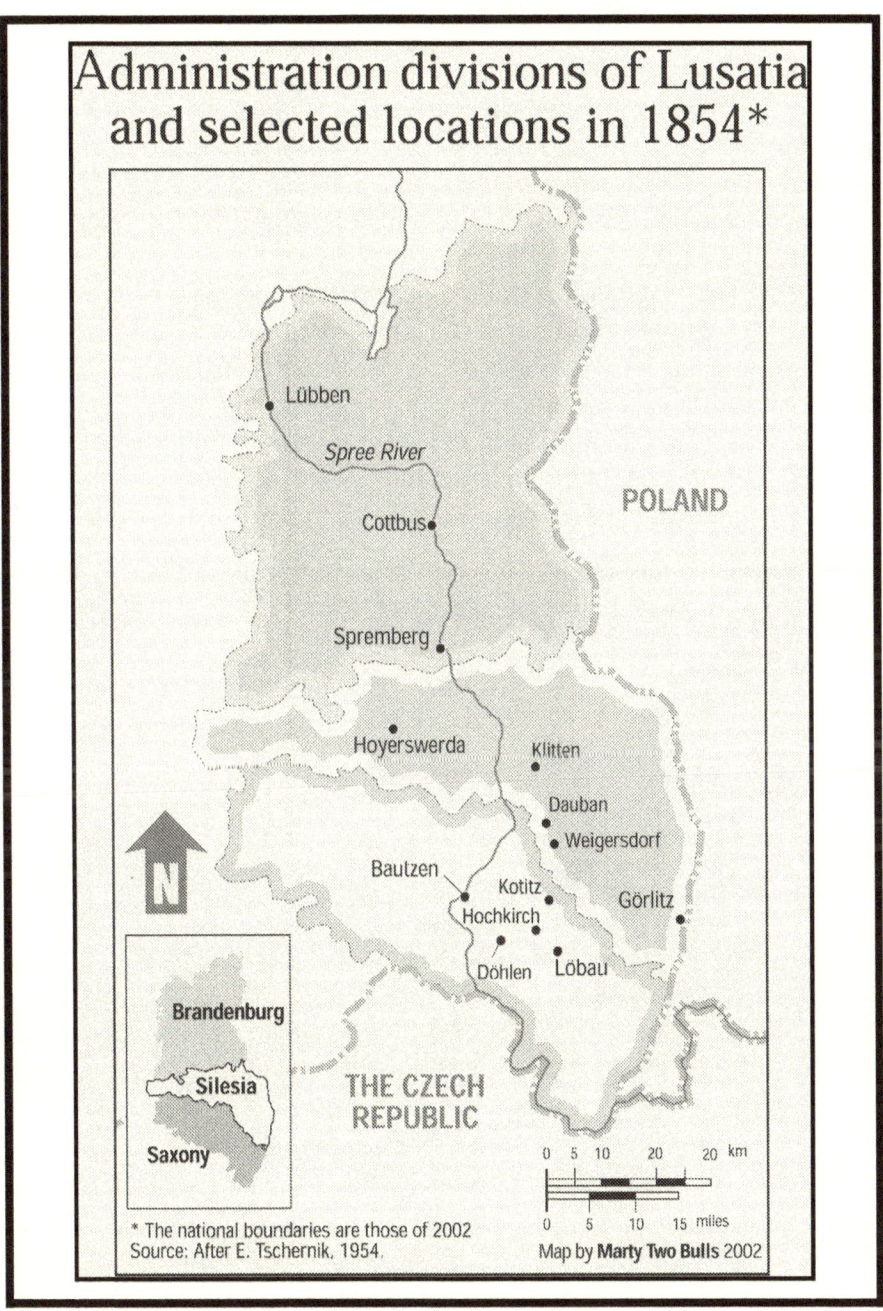

Map of Lusatia

the Germans had conquered the area and established German administrations and governments. Even though many Wends lost their lives in the protracted conflict or were assimilated by the Germans, many maintained their identity and by Kilian's time, some 250,000 were left living in Lusatia. Numerous villages remained predominately Wendish and there the Slavic culture, including the language, was perpetuated. The village where Kilian was born, Döhlen, was one of those villages.

Before the Napoleonic wars approximately 200,000 Wends lived in Saxony, but with the boundary change Saxony was left with only 50,000 and Prussia controlled 200,000. Prussia, in turn, divided its Wends and placed one portion under the administrative control of Brandenburg and one portion in the administrative unit of Silesia. As a result the Wends, unified in culture, were divided, if Saxony is included, under three different political structures.[3]

Döhlen birthplace and farm of Jan Kilian
Source: Trudla Malinkowa

During the same year when the area suffered from the devastation of the armies at the battle at Hochkirch, 1813, the youngster Johann suffered a personal loss when his mother, Maria Kilian nee Mättig, and his infant sister died. His grandmother, Agnes, came to help care for him until 1816, when his father, Peter Kilian, married again. Peter, called a *Freigartenbesitzer*, owned his home, attached agricultural buildings, and some land. But then in 1821, when Johann was ten, his father died. His grandmother also had died by this time, so he was taken to his grandfather's home at Hochkirch where he lived until he finished elementary school.[4] Because Johann was still a minor, Johann Mättig, his uncle and owner of a mill in Niethen, was made guardian. Johann inherited the family property and his uncle found a renter who leased the property and provided an income for the young orphan.

The psychological impact of all these deaths and uncertainties on the young child can be only a matter of speculation. The insecurity resulting from the losses could well have been compensated for by the security provided by an extended family. And all indications are that the family was devout and pious and from them Johann most likely learned about Christian living and faith in the resurrection. Yet it is almost impossible for Johann not to have retained some feeling of insecurity and in turn a need for reassurance and some basis of stability. Nevertheless, nothing in his writings indicate any anxiety during these early years.

The income from his father's property and support from his grandfather and uncle made secondary education a possibility. In 1826, at the age of fifteen, he became a student at the *Gymnasium* in Bautzen. Bautzen was the old fortress town on the Spree River and the administrative center for Upper Lusatia. It was only nine miles from Hochkirch. The *Gymnasium* in the German system of education was a program of secondary education which prepared students for university studies. The program of education was geared solely for males and for those individuals who could pass the entrance requirements and who wished to prepare themselves for a career in the professions. The Bautzen school took pride in its students, and many of its graduates became educational, political, and religious leaders. The goal, according to its mission statement, was to have each student become "a good, useful, contented, and successful person."[5]

Das alte Heim des Gymnasiums 1542 bis 1867

Bautzen Gymnasium
Source: Serbski Institut

The *Gymnasium*, located within the walls of Bautzen, had been founded in 1527. There were four classes during Kilian's time; Quarta, Tertia, Sekunda, and Prima. The size of each class varied between 33 and 50, while the size of the student body fluctuated between 185 and 233. More than one year could be spent during the final or Prima class, and it was not unknown for students to attend the *Gymansium* for six years. Kilian spent four and one-half years at the school.

The curriculum placed a heavy emphasis on languages, including Latin, Greek, Hebrew, French, and German. Latin was studied in each of the four classes, but German received the emphasis during the beginning years, while Greek and Hebrew received more attention during the later years. Wendish was not taught and Kilian's facility with the language was based on his instruction in grade school and his own study. Kilian and several other students who were interested in

Wendish formed a circle or club where they could communicate and study the language informally.[6]

Students did not live in a dormitory, but in private homes, often with a widow. Instruction began daily at 7 o'clock and ended at 4:00, with an hour break at noon. There was no instruction on Wednesday and Saturday afternoon. That free time could be used to attend private lectures, to participate in choirs, or to visit the town.[7] On Sunday the students could attend one of several churches, including Petridom for German or St. Michael, located outside the wall of the inner city, for Wendish services.

Having met the educational demands on the secondary level, Kilian entered the University of Leipzig in 1831 to study theology. Leipzig, in contrast to the regional center of Bautzen, was a city and an intellectual center boasting names such as J. S. Bach, Goethe, and Mendelssohn. The university was located near the center of the old city, near the church of St. Nicholas. Leipzig was also a center of Wendish nationalism—an intellectual movement which focused on the Wendish culture in contrast to the German.

Kilian was the thirtieth new student to register and did so on May 14, 1831. Eventually the number of new students reached 374. Within that number approximately 140 chose Theology or Theology/Philosophy as their course of study. Kilian paid his fees and gave his address as the fourth floor of Nicolaistrasse 753. During his four years at the university he shared his room with a classmate, Rudolph Richter.[8]

Just as in the Bautzen *Gymnasium*, there was a Wendish circle at Leipzig. The organization, called Sorabia, had been founded in 1716 by Wendish theology students and reorganized in 1814. It became the focal point in the wave of Wendish nationalism that flowered shortly before Kilian's attendance. Handrij Zejler, for example, matriculated at Leipzig in 1824, six years before Kilian, joined Sorabia and later became a pastor, a poet, and participant in the Wendish movement. But Kilian did not affiliate with Sorabia and instead associated with a German circle whose unifying goal was the preservation of pure Lutheran teaching. This decision was not a rejection of the Wendish culture, but was more likely an indication of Kilian's growing attraction to orthodox Lutheranism as a foundation in his life. It may also have been a reaction to the nature of the faculty–liberal and still heavily influenced by rationalism and the Enlightenment.[9]

Kilian completed his university studies when he successfully passed the prescribed final four-day examination *pro candidatura et pro licentia concionandi.* The document proclaiming his success, and dated March 31, 1835, licensed him to preach but did not make him eligible for a parish of his own. For that he needed two years of experience and yet another exam by church officials. His first position was in his home congregation at Hochkirch, where he became

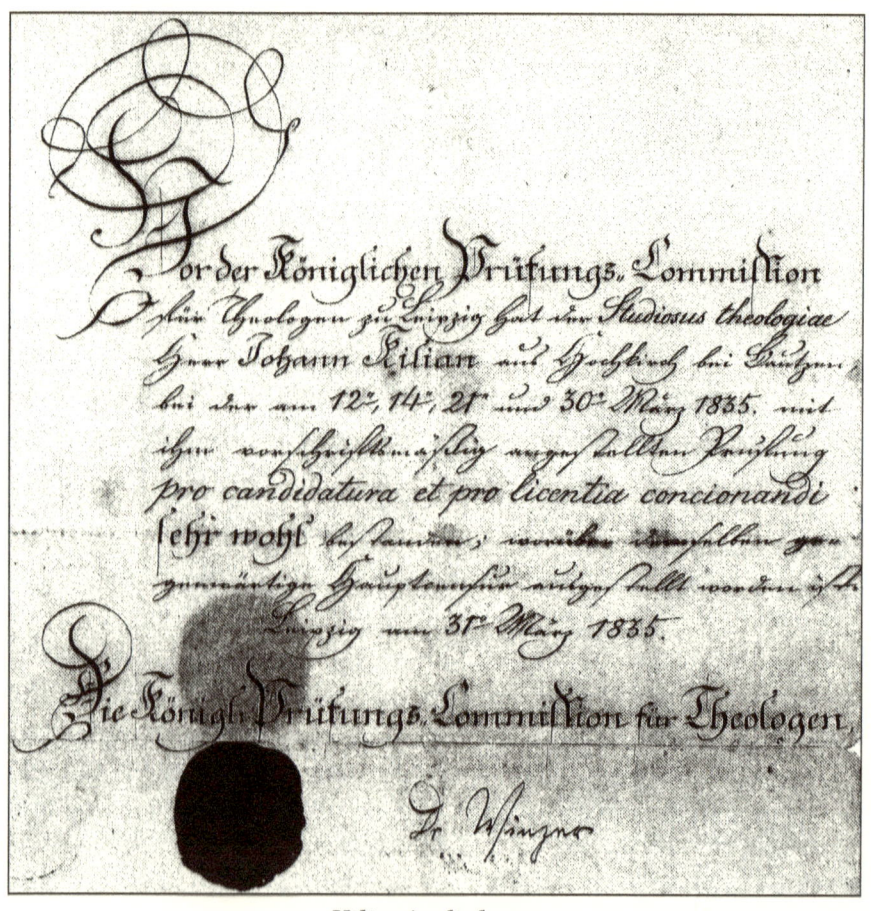

Kilian's diploma
Source: Texas Wendish Heritage Society

the assistant pastor. While most parishes were served by only a single pastor, some parishes which were large or parishes where the pastor's activity was restricted because of health or age, received an assistant pastor. The pastor, Michał Mjen, was middle-age, but Hochkirch was a large parish including many surrounding villages.

Then in December 1836 his uncle, Michael Kilian, pastor at Kotitz, just a few miles from Hochkirch, died, and Johann was encouraged to take the position. But before he would accept a parish Kilian still remembered a vow he had made in his youth to become a foreign missionary. So in the winter of 1837 he traveled to the Swiss city of Basel to learn more about a small mission school opened experimentally just the previous year. The school became a reality in 1840 and was called St. Chrischona. It grew in size and sent many missionaries to lands throughout the world. But the liberal philosophy of the state church was reflected in the emerging school and that did not match Kilian's Lutheran convictions, so he returned to Hochkirch.[10]

The position at Kotitz then became his choice, but before he could be considered he needed the certification of the Saxon church officials. Having waited for the required two years, he therefore readied himself for an examination and prepared a sermon which he would deliver before church officials in Dresden. He met that requirement on May 21, 1837. The next step was a demonstration sermon for the congregation. He delivered it on July 16. The final hurdle was winning the approval of the local nobleman and patron of the parish, Ernst Gottlob von Heynitz. That approval was given on September 8 and the ordination followed on September 24, nine months after the death of his uncle. At age twenty-six he completed his education and achieved his goal of being a pastor.[11]

KOTITZ

In contrast to agricultural practices in Texas, the farmers in Lusatia did not live in isolated homes constructed on their acreages and at a distance from their neighbors. Their homes were in villages and the farmers walked to their fields to tend them. The villages were sometimes located on hilly, less desirable land, along a brook. Within the villages existed not only the homes, but also barns, sheds, gardens, and orchards. The brook, the millpond, the trees on the slopes, and the animals all contributed to create a scene of rural tranquility. Because of the distance a person could walk to the fields was limited, the villages were generally small and not far apart.

As the establishment of a congregation for each village was unrealistic, several villages, over the centuries, joined to form a single parish. In one of the villages a church was built, often on the highest elevation, making its steeple visible for miles. The school also was associated with the church, so the farmers walked to their fields, the children walked to the school, and the family walked to the parish church on Sundays.

While many villages were assigned to the Hochkirch parish, only one village, Särka, belonged to the Kotitz parish. The small church building, constructed almost as a square with its steeple in the middle, was built in the 14th century. In its belfry hung a bell with the statement that testified to its Roman roots: *Maria hilf aus noth durch deines Kindes bittern Todt.*[12] During the Thirty Years' War, which preserved the region for the Lutheran faith, the church building suffered damage. But it was restored, and in the 21st century it still serves even though the ancient bell does not.

The new pastor took an interest not only in the spiritual life but also in the temporal life of his people. Kilian reported that in 1840 Kotitz numbered about ninety homes and the material conditions were generally improving. But there was also a segment of the population suffering from poverty, and that endangered the general welfare. Kotitz, like many other villages in Europe, was experiencing social change, and with it poverty, homelessness, drunkenness, and misery. One cause for this poverty and dislocation that also engulfed much of Europe can be traced to the end of feudalism. The serfs had been given their personal freedom and were released from their obligations, but many were in turn deprived of the land and houses they had occupied with the permission of the lord. They were free to make decisions and relocate, but some had no funds to enable them to purchase land or cottages. The lords also retained much of the land and instead of using resident serfs, hired seasonal workers. The landless workers

Kotitz church 1994
Source: J. Matschie

could earn an income during planting, harvest or threshing times, but
then there were periods of unemployment.

One proposed solution was the creation of Savings Unions or Associations of the Poor. These institutions encouraged people to save even a little bit for those times of unemployment. With the support of the local lord, Ernst Gottlob v. Heynitz, Kilian started a Society for the Poor (*Armenverein*) in 1845. It was less of a savings bank and more of a managed assistance program. The association was composed of a board of directors, a secretary, a treasurer, and two assessors. Kilian admitted that the handing out of welfare funds would not end drunkenness and wasteful spending, but the slovenly behavior needed to be stopped for the sake of the poor as well as for the parish in general.

Kotitz parsonage 2000
Source: Trudla Malinkowa

The directors also met every Friday evening to teach children skills through the formation of a straw-plaiting school and also a spinning school. Spinning was something family members could do at home to supplement household income. They bought the raw flax and then sold the linen thread. Neither idea worked and the poverty

Kilian observed in Kotitz increased. Some other solution was needed, and he even contemplated emigration as an option.[13]

Many Wends did not speak or could not read German, so Kilian, hoping to increase the piety of his people, also directed his attention to the translation of devotional material into Wendish, the mother tongue. The small size of his parish and an absence of family responsibilities enabled him to find time for his work. Already in 1838, Kilian published a sixty-seven page translation of Samuel Lucius, containing information for all who wished to be faithful Lutherans. Then in 1841 and 1842 three translations of Johann Phillip Fresenius appeared – one on the shepherds at Christmas, another on confession and Holy Communion, and the third on awakening and conversion. Two more translations followed: one in 1845, written by Johann Porst, on the steps toward hell or heaven; and finally, in 1847, Carl Bogatzky's popular devotional work.[14]

Kilian also realized the importance of religious music, and in 1846 he published a collection of twenty-eight songs – some translations from German, some his own compositions. The forty-page booklet was called "Songs of Joy." The initial publication contained only the words, but the next year he included the melodies. The booklet was used for decades in elementary schools and the last edition was published as late as 1881. The song book accomplished a double purpose. One was to enrich the religious life and the other was to strengthen the Wendish language. When Kilian prefaced the book, he said, "And if it is true, as some say, that the Wendish decline continues, then I present to you, dear Wendish brothers, this little songbook for your *good night* greeting, but if what they say is not true, then it can be your *good morning*." While his work in music most often dealt with translation of chorales from German into Wendish he also composed his own music and wrote original text. In all, he produced more than one-hundred hymns, and in the judgment of Gertrud Mahling, he deserves a place as one of the most productive Wendish evangelical poets.[15]

Eventually Kilian turned his efforts to the translations of the Lutheran confessions. While the devotional material appealed to the ordinary parishioner, much of the confessional material required concerted intellectual effort. Even today some of the words are strange for the ordinary person. The very word "confessions" in this context

George R. Nielsen

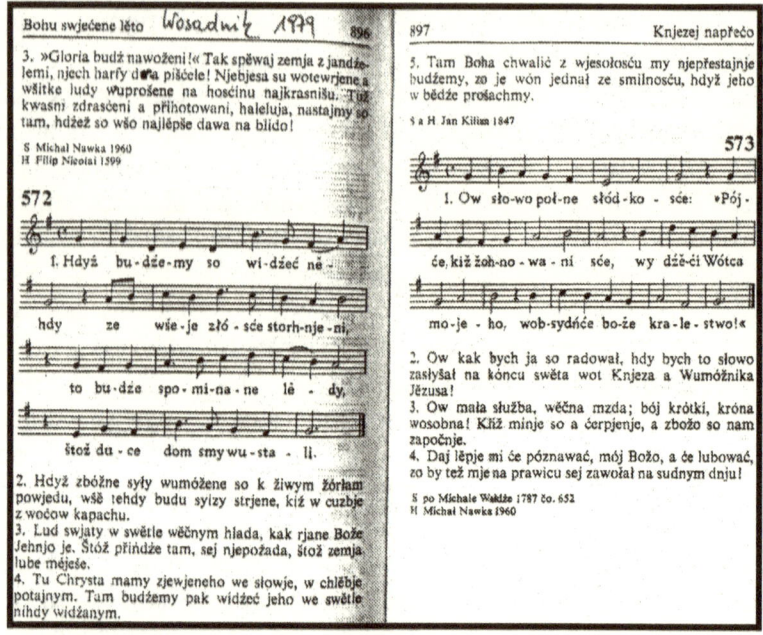

Kilian's hymn in a contemporary Catholic hymnal
Source: Serbski Institute

does not refer to admission of guilt, but to a series of documents that summarize, clarify, and explain items of doctrine or teachings of the church. Another word "symbolic" can also used when reference is made to the Lutheran confessions. Just as the symbol of the cross represents Christianity, so a creed or confession represents the truths of the Gospel.

There are seven Lutheran Confessions and they were written in the 16th century beginning with Luther's Small Catechism in 1529. The seven, along with the three creeds of the ancient church, were collected and published in 1580 in *The Book of Concord*. Kilian, starting in the late 1840s began translating and publishing one confession after another, until 1854 when all confessions were gathered and published in a single volume of 708 pages. Because the sale of the books would be insufficient to defray the publication costs, Johann Zwahr, a member of the parish of Gröditz, and the Wendish Evangelical Lutheran Societies which had been founded in 1849, gathered funds and supported the publication of these symbolical books. [16]

14

Wjeruwusnajerske pißma

aby

Symbolske knihi

evangelskeje lutherskeje zyrkwje,

po Lipsčanskim njemskim wudawku s ljeta 1766

pschetožene

wot

Jana Kiliana,

duchomneho w Wukrančizy.

Wojerezy,
čišchezane pola J. Kulmana.
1854.

Title page of the Lutheran Confessions
Source: Serbski Institute

During Kilian's years at Kotitz, his work with the Wendish language coincided with a broader movement that also had the goal of stimulating and enriching the Wendish language and culture. Wendish nationalism in its earliest stage had been dependent on a small number of pastors. Much akin to the American Civil Rights movement, where the leadership roles in the early years fell on the clergy by virtue of their education, so it was that the Wendish pastors were at the forefront of Wendish consciousness. Then as more Wends became educators, professionals, and journalists and the Wendish middle class grew in numbers, Wendish nationalism gained a broader base.[17]

The intellectuals who were part of the movement formed societies that promoted things Wendish and published journals on Wendish topics. One of these groups that Kilian joined was the Upper Lusatian Scientific Society in Görlitz, which although it was German, worked with Wendish folk songs and folk tales. The most prominent Wendish cultural and scientific association, *Maćica Serbska*, organized in 1847, included Kilian as a member. *Maćica Serbska* was dedicated to the growth and development of Wendish culture, letters, and publications. Although Kilian was part of the group, his participation in it was peripheral. Yet later in his life in Texas he corresponded with some of his fellow members.[18]

Kilian, however, disagreed with most of the prominent intellectuals who believed that the Wendish nationality and the Lutheran faith should not be linked because the joining of Lutheran faith with nationality would limit the support for Wendish nationality. Many of the Wendish intellectuals did not place such a high priority on the Lutheran faith as Kilian did and some of the Wends who supported the movement were Roman Catholic. Many, even though they themselves may have been pious, agreed that faith should be subordinated to Wendish interests. While Kilian was not ostracized by the intellectuals, he was never drawn into the inner circles. So they collected folk tales and folk songs and worked to enrich the Wendish culture, and Kilian implemented his belief that Wendish culture and the Lutheran faith were inseparable by translating religious works into the mother tongue to enrich the language and simultaneously nourish religious life.

Kilian also campaigned for the preservation of Wendish in the church when he worked with Lutheran groups. In 1844 he took part in a conference of the Saxon Bible Association in Dresden which was considering the publication of a new edition of the Wendish Bible. A German pastor of Bautzen opposed the endeavor and predicted the rapid demise of Wendish language. Kilian vehemently disagreed and supported the right of the Wends to read God's word in their native language. Even though the use of Wendish has declined over the years, the language survived and even though no new edition of the Bible appeared in 1844, other editions followed, the last one published in 1905.[19]

RELIGIOUS DISCONTENT

During his ministry at Kotitz, Kilian became involved with the controversies of Lutherans within their state churches – in both Saxony and Prussia. In Saxony there was discontentment because of the wavering supervision of the state church. Because the personal faith of the King of Saxony was Catholic, the leadership of the Lutheran Church of Saxony was placed under a consistory or group of clergymen. The enforcement of church teachings was not strict enough in the minds of many believers such as Kilian, and the administrators permitted a wide variety of religious views, especially those based on the philosophy of Rationalism. Rationalism, dominant in the previous century, continued to influence theological education and the clergy. This philosophy encouraged people to apply reason to situations in their lives. Miracles and articles of faith were rejected as not reasonable. Staunch Lutherans considered faith the foundation of their religious life and the Lutheran confessions a statement of their beliefs. They insisted on the practice that clergymen, at their ordination, would take the oath to uphold the Lutheran confessions.[20]

The spirit of Rationalism was also entrenched in the minds of many of the elementary teachers, and already in 1831 some tried unsuccessfully to free the schools from clergy influence. The school curriculum included religious instruction and the parish pastors supervised the elementary schools. In 1845 the teachers in the Saxon schools once again tried to detach themselves from the supervision of the clergy and sent petitions with 1,638 signatures to the legislative branch of the Saxon government. What followed was a tempest that flowed over into the Bautzen newspaper and involved a counter petition of thousands of farmers. Kilian asked a local judge, Andreas Wuchatsch, to write a petition opposing secularization and then obtained the endorsement of von Heynitz. It was called the Kotitz Petition, which 10,000 farmers eventually signed. In a letter to the newspaper, a correspondent complained that the petition had been circulated by lamplight and signatures gathered without proper information about the petition itself. In response, Wuchatsch acknowledged that he was the author, but that he was well acquainted with the symbolic books of the church and that he would never approve of any improper collection of signatures.

In a subsequent letter, another correspondent supported the petitions and explained that five clergymen had endorsed the petition, and that the petition had been presented in both German and Wendish. The petition, he added, contained nothing new, but attempted to keep the Lutheran Church of Saxony unchanged and protected against possible attacks. The legislature was sufficiently influenced and retained the union of church and school.[21]

The next year, 1846, one of the teachers who was active in the movement to secularize the schools, and also an intellectual, Johann Georg Melde of Grossdesha, not far from Hochkirch, wrote a document that led Kilian to believe that Melde rejected the Lutheran Confessions. Because Melde was expected to teach religion in school, Kilian joined in a lawsuit against Melde. The suit was unsuccessful and Melde continued to teach in his school. Even so, Kilian remained watchful and monitored teachers' meetings for renewed attempts to separate the schools from the church.[22]

Kilian's effectiveness in marshaling citizens on the school issue was duplicated in the pulpit, where he not only won the loyalty of his parishioners but also attracted listeners from the entire region. His sermons were vigorous and in 1845 he preached a sermon for Reformation Day that was published in both German and Wendish. It was titled "The Care Required of Lutheran Christians in the Present State of Confessional Confusion." In it he clearly stated the basis of the Lutheran faith and warned of threats to that faith within the state churches of Saxony and Prussia. It was distributed widely and applauded, and a German theological journal stated that if there were "a thousand pastors such as Kilian, evangelical Christianity would have a better future."[23]

In spite of these accomplishments, there was enough dissatisfaction with the religious climate as well as with the over-population and poverty in Saxony that many people turned to emigration. The migration to foreign lands revived Kilian's dream of foreign missions and he viewed the migration and the religious freedom arising in the world as God's way of opening the doors for evangelism. Kilian thought of alternatives to parish service and worried that these doors for foreign missions could also close. Many Germans from neighboring Silesia, a province controlled by Prussia, were migrating to Australia. They were Old Lutherans, and held religious views much like his, so perhaps he could be a pastor for those people and serve as a missionary to the native people at the same time. In 1844 he discussed the advantages and disadvantages of migration with the Old Lutheran leaders in Breslau, a town in Silesia.[24]

Kilian wrote, "In overpopulated Saxony, one must, who thinks of the future, consider migration as a goal of salvation, when the harsh results of overpopulation become so painful, as I encounter in Kotitz year in and year out. Yet one needs an external motive and a good prospect."[25]

The next year in 1845 Kilian initiated a correspondence with Pastor A. L. C. Kavel, who had already migrated from Silesia to Australia in 1838. Kilian contemplated joining Kavel's Australian group with a number of Wends, but he was uncertain whether the Wends could establish a Wendish village and maintain their cultural identity. He must have resolved his concern because he opened negotiations with an agent, Edward Delius in Bremen, for a ship that would travel to Australia. Kilian also corresponded with Pastor Phillip Oster, a German from Posen, who would travel with his congregation to Australia in 1847.[26] Kilian, however, took no further actions and no source has been found revealing the reasons why Kilian did not pursue his plans. Quite possibly there was an insufficient number of Wends who wished to migrate, or he realized the impracticality of his dreams. Under either circumstance, his actions do indicate some level of unrest.

A final project Kilian envisioned in an attempt to save the Saxon church was the creation of a monthly journal for Wendish Lutherans. Already in May 1842, he proposed this journal that would include articles on interpretations of Scripture, church doctrine, church history, and also hymns and poems. His proposed title was "Testimony of God's Church: Published for the Edification of Wends." But before he could embark on the project it was necessary for him to apply to the Saxon Ministry of Culture for a license. His application, however, was rejected and Kilian was not given the reason for his rejection. An internal memo from the Saxon officials in Bautzen to the Ministry in Dresden reported that Kilian had been watched and they viewed him as being "somewhat fanatical" and assumed that his motives were to reach beyond his parish and to give nourishment to the conventicles.

Five years later, in August 1847, he reapplied for the license but changed the journal's title to "The Monthly Paper of the Wendish Lutheran Church." The results were identical. Kilian was embittered and speculated that the reason for his rejection was either the Lutheran emphasis, the promotion of the Wendish language and identity, or Kilian himself. Even before his rejection had arrived, Kilian was beginning to shift his attention away from Saxony and across the border to Prussia.[27]

While Kilian did what he could to hinder the growth of liberalism and secularism in the Saxon church, the Saxon faithful responded in a different manner. Their response was through the use of conventicles or prayer meetings. This tradition can be traced to the practices of the Moravian Brethren and also to Pietism. Attending church and participating in the sacraments constituted a basic requirement for Christians, but pious people sought to extend religion to the other days of the week. They met in private homes, without the presence of clergymen, for study, singing hymns, and praying. Their focus was on the heart. Kilian, himself had grown up in a pious family, but as he was an educated clergyman, his focus was on the head. Kilian tolerated the conventicles and did not support them, even though many of his writings were read at the meetings. Within the meetings the faithful could ignore the liberal tendency of the church and practice religion their way. So they remained within the Saxon state church because the Saxon government abdicated its role in the structure of the church and the pietists could supplement their religious life to suit themselves.[28]

In neighboring Prussia, however, the king exercised his temporal power over the religious realm. Although the majority of Prussia's citizens were Protestant, one portion followed the teachings of Luther and the other the teachings of Calvin. King Frederick William III, in 1817, desired a single unified state church, so he worked to bring a union between the Lutherans and Calvinists. If he were to accomplish that goal, the differences that existed between the two bodies would be suppressed and the common ground would be highlighted. The liturgy was modified and written in such general terms so that neither faith would disagree. Sermons focused on non-controversial matters. In the early years the program constituted of nothing more than a gentle pressure on the congregations and clergy. But then in 1830 the king decreed the Union into existence.

In various parts of Prussia, especially in the province of Silesia, there was a dissatisfaction with the religious blend. The Lutherans who objected to this arrangement were called Old Lutherans and the government exercised extensive pressure and some persecution to force them to comply. Many did not choose to do it, so they turned to migration to Australia or America, where they could practice their Lutheran faith without state interference. The dissatisfaction and unrest was sufficiently intense, so that in 1841 the new king, Frederick William IV made some concessions. Those individuals who wished could form independent congregations, without state regulation and without subsidy.[29]

Kilian sympathized with the Old Lutherans in Silesia, but he did not become involved until some Wends living in that part of Lusatia that had become Prussian with the Congress of Vienna, joined in the protest. But this involvement, slight as it might have been, was the step onto the stage that would draw him into a scenario as preordained as a Greek play. The first objection among the Wends against the Union church began in the early 1840s shortly after the concessions were made. In the village of Weigersdorf, one mile from the Saxon border, in the Gross Radisch parish, Andreas Urban, the village shoemaker had traveled to Spremberg to buy leather and learned about the project of the king. He and other Weigersdorf people then realized that their pastor, without mentioning anything, had been introducing the state-approved liturgy into the church services. With the help of their teacher, Andreas Dutschmann, they convinced their pastor to return to the Lutheran liturgy. But soon the pastor reversed himself and used the United Agenda.[30]

The consciences of the people at Weigersdorf were troubled because they were participating in a sacrament where the liturgy and words of institution did not adhere to their Lutheran teachings. It was not so much a matter of what was said as of what was left unsaid. Lutherans walk a narrow line in the Lord's Supper between the promise of "life and salvation" for those who take the sacrament worthily, but "death and damnation" for those who take it unworthily. The sacrament is a serious matter.[31] Urban frequently traveled to Saxony to worship in the Lutheran churches there, and one of those churches was Kilian's church in Kotitz. Urban's brother even migrated to Saxony. But others, including Teacher Dutschmann, began studying the writings of the Old Lutherans and consulted with Kilian. After Kilian translated the writings into Wendish and explained the arguments of the Old Lutherans, as well as the doctrinal implications, the awakened Prussians realized that in order to calm their consciences, they could no longer participate in the Prussian church and needed to form an independent Lutheran congregation.[32] The Saxon solution of conventicles was not an option, because the sacraments could only be performed by ordained clergymen, and performing the sacrament at the conventicles was out of the question.

The separatists called for help from the Old Lutherans, and Pastor Gessner from Freystadt in Lower Silesia offered to serve them. Gessner himself was a staunch Lutheran and had spent five years in jail for his opposition to the United church. The new congregation was organized on May 1, 1843 with fourteen people from Weigersdorf and the neighboring village of Klitten and the *Oberkirchenkollegium zu Breslau*, the umbrella organization for the Old Lutherans, accepted the new congregation into its fold. Gessner traveled there every three months and the group in Weigersdorf met at Urban's house while the group in Klitten met with the Lehnig family in neighboring Ölsa.[33]

The religious discontent with the United church spread to the neighboring areas and membership increased. The people at Weigersdorf hoped to install Kilian as their pastor, and shortly after the formation of the congregation, Kilian agreed to become their pastor under two conditions. The congregation would need to pledge that it would remain faithful to the pure Lutheran beliefs and also he would need a permit from Prussian authorities to immigrate. While the permit was being processed, Gessner, on May 18, 1844, named Kilian as his deputy at Weigersdorf.

But there was opposition to Kilian's participation with the Old Lutherans both in Prussia and in Saxony. In Prussia some pastors who were cooperating with the Prussian Union, feared the growing popularity of the separatists and that Kilian's presence would strengthened them, composed a statement accusing Kilian of agitation and creating unrest. As a result the Prussian authorities denied his request for Prussian citizenship and the Saxon authorities threatened Kilian with removal from office and prohibited him from working in the neighboring country. The Wendish newspaper editor and leading intellectual, Jan Arnošt Smoler, questioned the entire movement that could be started when shoemakers and ordinary people were preaching and creating confusion, and he was saddened by Kilian's participation. Yet he promised to withhold judgment for a while and found Kilian's concern for the Wends a redeeming element in an otherwise undesirable situation.

In spite of government interference and the absence of a full-time clergyman, membership in the Weigersdorf/Klitten group increased, and a home in another village, Dauban, became a meeting place. Weigersdorf had the largest cluster, but because the membership was scattered and the distances substantial, they decided to build two small churches, one at Weigersdorf and one at Klitten. Even though the Prussia church policy had mellowed, and construction was allowed, some restrictions remained. Neither building, in keeping with the law, could include a steeple. The church at Weigersdorf was dedicated on December 20, 1846, and the one at Klitten eleven months later.[34]

The Prussian government eventually reversed its ruling toward Kilian and the authorities agreed to permit Kilian to serve the two congregations on the condition that he would not create unrest or proselytize. The Kotitz patron, von Heynitz, as well as the church authorities in Bautzen, also gave their permission, so beginning in June 1847 Kilian served both the Saxon and Prussian churches and in October he participated in the dedication of the Klitten church. This strenuous schedule continued for about a year until he accepted a call to Prussia, and on St. Michael's Day of 1848 he vacated his position in Kotitz and settled at Dauban – geographically between Weigersdorf and Klitten.

On several occasions Kilian tried to explain the options that he considered in making that final step. And certainly there were times when he regretted making it. Kotitz remained in his memory as the most satisfying time of his life. He went because no one else was willing to go. A young Wend, a recent graduate of the seminary, had turned down the call from the separatists, and the presence of a pastor was important if the little flock were to grow. Kilian knew that a replacement for him at Kotitz in the Saxon state church could be found, but obtaining a pastor for a small independent congregation was another matter. His conscience told him to go where he was needed the most.[35] But it was a fateful step and it locked him into a course of which he did not know the ending.

At Kotitz Kilian had security as a pastor in the state church, and his congregation was free of religious controversy. He had time for creative activity. If there was conflict, as he engaged in preserving the Wendish minority culture in the context of German majority and as he worked to uphold the Lutheran tradition in a secular and rationalist setting, it was on his own terms. In his next ministry outside the state church he would enjoy little economic security. His scattered flock demanded his attention and there was little time for creativity. Preservation of the Wendish culture was no longer the priority, but the focus of his ministry was the survival of the Lutheran tradition in conflict with state-supported Protestantism.

WEIGERSDORF AND KLITTEN

The year 1848, when Kilian made the transition from Saxony to Prussia, was a tumultuous time in Germany and much of Europe. Revolutions, led by liberal and nationalistic proponents called for a national parliament and a constitution for a united Germany. The

Wends in Saxony, largely untouched by the turmoil, professed their loyalty to the king, and Kilian's attention was not distracted from his provincial activity.

Maria Gröschel Kilian
Source: Texas Wendish Heritage Society

Kilian, still a bachelor, moved his possessions to a farmer's house in Dauban. He lived there from 1848 until the Weigersdorf parsonage was completed in 1852. In the fall of 1848 he married Maria Gröschel, a member of his Kotitz congregation and twelve years his junior. She was the eldest daughter of a small landowner in Särka, Andreas Gröschel, who later with his four other children, joined the young couple in the migration to Texas. The wedding took place in Weigersdorf and a personal friend, a candidate for the ministry, Jaroměr H. Imiš preached the sermon. Of the four children that Maria bore in Europe, only one, Gerhard, would survive into maturity.[36]

Instead of stepping into an established parish as he had done in Kotitz, Kilian first needed to organize a parish, one that was not based on geographical boundaries but on boundaries of faith. The new parish included the Lutherans of Weigersdorf and Klitten, as well as members scattered throughout Prussian Lusatia in eighteen different villages and included such towns as Spremberg, Muskau, and Cottbus. He divided his Sundays evenly between the two primary congregations, but every quarter he went on a tour to the other members. The tour lasted three weeks. He preached in both Wendish and German, and when he was not present a layman led the service and read the sermon. In his travels, Kilian was assisted by a farmer from Dauban, Carl Teinert, who served as the chauffeur as well as the song leader or cantor.

In addition to traveling and preaching, Kilian met the state requirement for keeping records of the membership and reporting them. Because of the haphazard nature of pastoral attention prior to his arrival, Kilian had to sort out the membership and initiate records. He still had not completed the task by 1850. The impressive growth in membership was a happy complicating cause. Only fourteen people had been present at the formation of the group in 1843 and by 1852 there were 1200 members. And when members of a state church joined with Kilian, Kilian was required to formally notify the pastor of the state church by time-consuming letters.[37]

Yet another task of taking charge of the new parish was establishing a rapport with the clergymen as well as the police and officials of the communities where members of Kilian's flock lived. State officials could not be expected to simplify the life of a dissident

Weigersdorf Church (Contemporary)
Source: Andreas Otto

pastor, and local clergymen were neither pleased with the competition nor with the potential for controversy the Old Lutherans introduced. Early on there were incidents that complicated Kilian's efforts and consumed his time.

In 1848, for example, Kilian received a notice from Reichwalde officials that he had conducted a burial that had not been announced by the village pastor. One of the guidelines required that certain official acts were to be announced from the state church pulpits, even though they were to be performed by an independent pastor. Then in 1849, Kilian was called on by an Old Lutheran family in the Schleife parish to baptize their child. However, before the sacrament could take place, the village pastor appeared with the village police and drove Kilian away from the congregation. The members then fled to Tzschelln seven miles away and there the child was baptized. In all of these incidents endless correspondence ensued in which Kilian clarified himself, justified himself, and demanded that the pastors and government officials recognize the Old Lutheran congregations and their pastor.[38]

In time, Kilian's relationship with the state clergymen warmed and some pastors even intimated their support of the Lutheran confessions while retaining their positions within the state church. Yet Kilian refused to accept their statements as sincere and pointed out the impossibility of harmonizing the two. A church, he insisted, was held together by its confessions, and not by state power or church property. Lutherans, or as he said, "captive Lutherans," could exist within the state church, but such persons were no more Lutheran than a Prussian serving under a French general was a Prussian. Being a Lutheran in Prussia publicly was impossible within the state church.[39]

In addition to the pressures from outside the congregation, there were also problems inside. State churches received state funds but the Old Lutheran congregations received none. The debts incurred from the construction of the churches, the school, and parsonage weighed heavily on members whose finances were modest to begin with. The financial future of the congregation and Kilian's own were bleak. In 1850 he said, "It is my misfortune that I came to Prussia. I do not believe that our congregations can hold on much longer."[40]

Parsonage at Weigersdorf
Source: Andreas Otto

Spiritually there were problems. Some of the devout, once they separated themselves from the state church, adopted an arrogant attitude that they alone were the chosen ones and that the others had compromised their faith by remaining. That attitude, and the large number of the usual practical problems, prevented total attention to the vital matters of faith. Kilian at times wondered if the separation had been too hasty, or even necessary, and that the separation resulted from nothing more than human pride. He looked to Elijah's actions in the Bible and to the reform movements in history, such as the Waldensians and Luther, for guidance.[41]

Other than admitting error or defeat and closing the congregation, Kilian had another option – emigration. Australia had attracted Kilian's attention already when he was looking for an alternative to the problems at Kotitz. Now at Weigersdorf, in 1851, he again was reminded of migration because his staunch supporter from Saxony, Johann Zwahr, was organizing a group bound for Australia which included Andreas Urban, chairman of the Weigersdorf congregation.

Kilian discussed the possibility with the Old Lutheran pastor, Ludwig Otto Ehlers, in Liegnitz. Kilian proposed that he would serve the Wends in Australia as their pastor and also work with the Aborigines. Ehlers, however, believed that the two could not be combined and that Kilian would be obligated to choose between them. Ehlers also believed that many more Wends would stay in Germany than would migrate to Australia and that it would be an impossibility to maintain Wendish identity with the few who did migrate.[42]

While the six years in Prussia must have been exhausting, they were by no means a failure. The congregations had grown to a size large enough, so that when the migration took place, they absorbed the loss and survived. And Kilian also completed the final tasks associated with his translation of *The Book of Concord* and *Luther's Large Catechism,* both published in 1854, the year of migration.

PREPARING FOR MIGRATION

Even though a large number of Germans from Silesia had migrated to Australia with Kavel, no groups of Wends migrated there until 1848. During that year, 1848, two groups from Upper Lusatia sailed, one of which included Pastor Andreas Kappler from Weissenberg and the other led by Michael Deutscher a vocal critic of the teachers who wished to secularize the schools. Three years later, in 1851, Zwahr and his group departed. This is the group that hoped to lure Kilian and the group Kilian referred to later in Texas.

Australia ceased being the destination for their migration in the summer of 1853 when seven Wendish families numbering thirty-five people left from the Bautzen train station for Texas. This group was made up of Wends, all from Prussian villages and all holding the same religious views as Kilian. Their decision to migrate to Texas instead of Australia was based on the shorter passage, the less expensive travel, and negative reports from Australia and the conditions there.

Once individuals of this group had settled in Texas, they wrote favorable letters home to Lusatia, and the Wends turned their thoughts away from Australia and toward Texas. Kilian reported that a total of five letters had been received in Germany and that they were passed around. The number of people interested in migrating increased, and on March 25, 1854, in compliance with government regulations, some laymen filed for a charter with the state officials at Liegnitz to form an association. The home of the association was Dauban, and the officers and leaders were Carl Lehman, Carl Teinert, Ernst Adolph Moerbe, Johann Hohle, Christoph Kokel, and Johann Urban. In May they sent Kilian the call to be their pastor. The Old Lutheran administration tried to convince Kilian to reject the call because he was the only Wendish pastor in Prussia and was indispensable for the care of the Weigersdorf/Klitten congregation. Pastor Ehlers, pastor at Liegnitz and superintendent, wrote to Kilian and also visited him, but without success.[43]

The emigrant association realized that many of their friends, neighbors, and congregation members also desired to migrate but could not because of a lack of funds. They decided that they would assist the poor by contributing one-fourth of their possessions to the treasury and collected 8,000 Taler. As a result 558 persons, including 170 children, began preparations for the journey.[44]

In anticipation of constructing a church, the leaders ordered a bell from the foundry at Kleinwelka with the inscription "Gottes Wort und Luthers Lehr vergehet nun und nimmermehr."[45] There were no laws in Texas against steeples. Kilian packed his books and decided to take his carriage. The contract for transportation was signed with Valentin Lorenz Meyer. The leaders, acting on the advice of the 1853 immigrants, insisted on Hamburg as the exit port rather than Bremen.

As the members of the group sold their possessions and made preparations, the news of the migration drew the attention of the countryside, the press, and the government officials. The newspapers ran notices warning them of the dangers ahead and the dangers of the journey. Government officials, worried about losing citizens, had the association charter translated from Wendish into German and attended the association meetings, to see whether any laws were being broken. Unable to find wrong-doing in the association, there were judicial inquiries against individuals. Kilian, himself, was charged in a suit by a father of one of his migrants for inciting someone to emigrate.

In spite of all the opposition, the group of 531 emigrants gathered at the Bautzen train station on September 4, 1854. Journalists from as far away as Leipzig reported the event. One reporter described the people as "in the prime of their years, upstanding, healthy, and strong; and judging from their clothing, impressive, progressive peasants and artisans, of which some are supposedly well off and have pledged to carry the travel costs of their poor companions..." The reason for the migration was to found a colony in Texas, "where they can be undisturbed, which they allege did not happen here in the former fatherland, and there adhere to the besieged old faith and Luther's pure teaching." Kilian's suit at the Royal Prussian Circuit Court at Rothenburg, however, had not been resolved so even though he was present at the station, he could not board the train.[46]

When the group arrived in Hamburg on September 5th, the leaders inspected the ships and discovered that the largest ship in the port could accommodate no more than 300 individuals and that was too small even without the stragglers who would join them soon. Meyer proposed dividing the group but the leaders had envisioned traveling as a single group and would not consider Meyer's proposal. Meyer then suggested that they travel to Liverpool where there were larger ships, even though Meyer's profit would be reduced. So after seven days at Hamburg waiting for stragglers and baggage, 555 people crossed the North Sea by steamship to Grimsby, England and then by train to Liverpool.[47]

KILIAN'S LEADERSHIP AND THE VOYAGE

A commemorative marker placed by the state of Texas near the entrance of the Serbin church reads, "Here in 1854 Under The Leadership of Rev. John Kilian Ev. Luth. Pastor About 600 Wends Seeking Religious Liberty Established The First Wendish Settlement in Texas". Other than missing the date by one year and slightly overstating the emigrant number, one could question the claim of leadership for Kilian. Many other books and articles on the Wends, including *The New Handbook of Texas*, also credit Kilian with leading the group. To some extent that usage is a form of shorthand substituting "leadership" for "prominence." But it is misleading and blurs Kilian's role. Who were the real leaders of the migration and what was the actual nature of Kilian's leadership?

Even though Kilian considered migration as a solution to problems as far back as his time in Kotitz, there is no documentation that he proposed the idea of migration to his Weigersdorf parish or promoted it with his parishioners. Instead the formulators of the idea and the leaders were laymen who established an Emigration Association. A sufficient number of people expressed their interest in migration so that the leaders sent a call to Kilian to accompany them as their pastor. This attempt at taking a pastor along was not a new idea either. Johann Zwahr tried, without success, to do it in 1851. When Kilian accepted the call, he did not become the leader of the migration, he became the "religious leader."[48] Even his call did not give him job security. It had an escape clause of one year in the event that the attempt of founding a congregation was not successful.

While the lay leaders organized the migrants into groups and boarded the train for Hamburg, Kilian remained behind. Once the court cleared him of the charge and his permit to migrate was returned to him, he took his wife and two-year-old son and left on September 13 for Hamburg. The main party waited at Hamburg for some other families, but departed for England before dawn on the morning of the 12th, two days before Kilian arrived. In an attempt to join the group, Kilian followed advice to change his route to make up for time lost. Instead of waiting for a ship to cross the North Sea, Kilian left his luggage at Hamburg and boarded the train for Cologne. The route would take him through Belgium and across the channel at Dover and then on to London and Liverpool.

Sadly the plan failed because just after the train had cleared Belgium customs at Verviers, and was beginning to move, Kilian noticed that his passport had not been returned. Then that evening at Mecheln, in the crowded conditions, Kilian was separated from his family, and Mrs. Kilian and Gerhard were on a car for Brussels, and he, thinking it was going to Ghent, boarded a car for Ghent. When he arrived at Ghent he was assisted by a Flemish person who found Mrs. Kilian at Antwerp and returned with her to Ghent. He also went to police for help to retrieve his pass. They found it difficult to believe that one person could lose his pass and his family on the same day, but they sent a letter to Verviers and a few days later the pass arrived.[49]

Kilian finally arrived at Liverpool on September 20, a full week after the others. While the *Ben Nevis*, a ship large enough to carry 689 passengers, more than enough space for the entire group, was being readied for the voyage to Galveston, the emigrants were housed in boarding houses. When he arrived, several people had already died of cholera. Before they left Liverpool, fourteen people died in the port.

Even though the records do not mention Kilian's participation in the burials, he did conduct several worship services in Liverpool, both in German and Wendish. He preached on Saturday, September 23, on the assumption that the voyage would begin. He could not finish the service because disruptive sailors started singing. The ship did not sail, so the next day, Sunday, Kilian conducted services in the morning and communion services in the afternoon. There was another service on Monday, the eve of the departure, and also on Tuesday afternoon, September 26, as the ship sailed west.

But eight more people died during the next days, so on September 29 the captain steered the ship to Queenstown, Ireland. Many immigrants were disappointed with the delay that eventually would last for three weeks, but at least ten of the Wends who had been hospitalized at Liverpool, could rejoin the group. The sick were taken to a hospital ship and the healthy went on board the old frigate the *Inconstant* while the *Ben Nevis* was disinfected and cleaned and the bedding destroyed. Even though the passengers were restricted to the ship for three weeks, they ate well. Fresh wheat bread and milk arrived every day and fresh meat, specially prepared for the German palate, was prepared every other day.[50]

During those three weeks, Kilian conducted Wendish and German services on Sundays, and devotions, from time to time. As the days dragged on, and people grew impatient, Kilian received an anonymous letter criticizing him for neglecting his office and not teaching the children during the idle hours. Kilian gave the letter to the lay leaders and they came to his defense and rebuked the unknown author for the unchristian-like manner in which he had expressed himself. No formal document or constitution regulating the school had been drafted so Kilian could not be blamed. Yet in order to formalize some sort of leadership, they elected a council of five men – two Saxons and three Prussians.[51]

Contract for cabin on Ben Nevis
Source: University of Texas Archives

Finally, on October 23, the ship left Queenstown and began its seven and one-half week voyage to Texas. Kilian and his family occupied a cabin, for an additional cost of 254 Taler, while the congregation traveled in the hold. During the voyage Kilian continued the Sunday church services in Wendish and German, periodic evening devotions, and on Tuesday, October 31, observed the Festival of Reformation. He even instructed and confirmed some children. There were two storms, one shortly after the departure from Ireland and one violent one in the Gulf of Mexico. Kilian, in letters to Walther and Dutschmann, wrote that there were no storms, but in his diary Kilian referred to the winds on one occasion as being strong and unfavorable and that everything in the hold fell topsy-turvy. They arrived at Galveston on December 16 after the loss of seventy-four persons.[52]

Kilian, on one occasion, did indeed refer to himself as the leader of the migration. In an 1859 letter to a pastor in Australia, Kilian compared himself to Moses and pointed out that even Moses suffered from divisiveness. On one specific occasion on the voyage when cholera continued to threaten and when the people were huddled below deck suffering from sea-sickness, the captain insisted that the passengers come on deck for their own good. Not everyone cooperated and the captain threatened to use his sailors to physically drag the noncompliers up. Kilian intervened and used persuasion to accomplish the same result. Kilian, however, noticed that there was some resentment toward his intervention and believed that a controversy which surfaced four years later had its roots in this event. The incident, instead of bolstering Kilian's claim of leadership can be used as an example to show that Kilian had limits and when he exceeded his religious responsibilities he caused resentment.[53]

When the ship was safely at anchor, Kilian and his family, eager to rest on terra firma, left the ship and spent the first night in Texas in a Galveston hotel, leaving the management of customs inspection and further transportation to the lay leaders.

2
KILIAN IN TEXAS 1854-1884

The bell of the stone church near Serbin signaled a death at 11:00 o'clock on that morning of September 12, 1884. That bell, a symbol of faith and an instrument in worship, had crossed the ocean with the immigrants in 1854 and was installed in a bell tower three years later. People within earshot stopped what they were doing and listened as its peals reached seventy-five. Then after a pause, the bell resumed again, and finally after yet another pause there followed a third set of seventy-five. The third set of seventy-five completed the code and announced the death of a confirmed member of the congregation.[1] In such a close-knit community everyone knew who was advanced in age and who was suffering from illness, and they speculated whose death had been announced. This time it tolled for their pastor, Johann Kilian.

Ever since his wife's death three years earlier, Kilian had weakened physically and even predicted that he would die unexpectedly. Even so, he loved preaching, and just the previous Sunday he had climbed the familiar steps to the pulpit.[2] Kilian had been a vital force in the life of the congregation and had raised his voice at innumerable funerals of his flock – even before they had migrated to Texas. Now his voice was silent and the bell signaled the end of his journey and also an end of his mission.

The next day members of the congregation and friends gathered in the austere white church to honor his life and service. As they passed through the double doors under the tower on the west end of the building, the men and boys turned and ascended the steps to the balcony that formed a U shape while the women and children continued to the benches in the nave. The interior, also relatively plain, revealed walls painted white and a ceiling that was sky blue. Light streamed in through the four tall, narrow windows on each side, making artificial illumination unnecessary. Opposite the entrance was the pulpit, centered and raised to the level of the balcony while above the entrance, on the same level as the pulpit, was the Trayser Harmonium, a large reed organ. The assembly sang the hymns of death and resurrection and listened to the Rev. Carl Geyer offer words of comfort and trust to the bereaved just as Johann Kilian had done so many times.

The Kilian family 1868 – Gerhard was in Addison, Illinois
Source: Texas Wendish Heritage Society

The immediate family included the eldest son, Gerhard, who as a two-year-old had migrated with his parents to Texas in 1854. After studying under his father's direction, Gerhard was sent, at the tender age of fifteen, to the Lutheran Teacher's Seminary at Addison, Illinois, in 1867. A pastor, C. T. H. Fick of Collinsville, Illinois, had been in Serbin to visit the congregation and escorted Gerhard to St. Louis, where he then stayed with C. F. W. Walther until someone could take him to Addison.[1] The school, in its infancy, having been founded in 1864, was patterned after the German *Gymnasium* with four years of secondary education and one year of college. After Gerhard completed his five years in 1872, he assumed his father's position as teacher of the congregation's school. Church music had been part of the curriculum, and he became an accomplished organist and an enthusiastic leader in singing the familiar Wendish hymns. His father was especially pleased with Gerhard's ability at playing the foot pedals.

After his installation as teacher, Gerhard gained permission to partition off the east end of the old frame church for his residence. When the stone church had been completed, the frame church became the school, but only a portion of the building was really needed for educational purposes. The new arrangement enabled him to obtain privacy, but it also relieved the pressure from the crowded parsonage. When he was single, Gerhard walked to the parsonage for his meals. Gerhard soon married a Wendish girl from the neighborhood, in 1874, but after six years of marriage, she died shortly after the birth of her third child. Gerhard's second wife was also a Wend from the Serbin community, and before Pastor Kilian's death the couple added one more grandchild for the grandfather to baptize.

Theresia Martha, age twenty-seven, sat with her husband of eight years, Johann Albert Peter. She also had attended the school taught by her father, and was clearly her father's favorite. The father considered her a gifted child and claimed that she was reading before the age of one. She learned German as a second language and even aspired to learn English. Because of her mother's frequent illnesses, Theresia early in life, assumed the duties of a homemaker and also became an accomplished seamstress and milliner. Even though she did not dance

39

Kilian and Theresia 1876
Source: Texas Wendish Heritage Society

or flaunt herself, she was pleasant and popular and Kilian was fearful for her future. He saw no one in Texas that was good enough for her and hoped that she would marry an educated person rather than a farmer or businessman from the community. When she was twenty years old, she did marry a local businessman who owned a steam mill, and he was not even Wendish, but German. Her departure from the parsonage was a sad event for Kilian, but at least she stayed in the neighborhood and he would live to baptize four of her children.[2]

Bernhard, age twenty-six, a farmer and craftsman, sat with his new bride, Anna Maria Schulze. In contrast to his brothers, he was not interested in academic subjects, and Kilian admitted that he could not fathom Bernard's disposition. He loved to whittle, and his younger siblings surpassed him in school. As he knew he wanted to work with his hands, he received training in cabinet making from Pastor J. A. Proft at Fedor, who had also designed and constructed the windows of the stone church. Making a living in Lee County solely from woodworking was not realistic, and Bernard considered going north to Fort Wayne, where his younger brother was studying. But he stayed and took up farming as his primary activity and woodworking became a secondary source of income. Kilian eventually resigned himself to Bernard's occupational interests and was satisfied that Bernard maintained a Christian life and associated with Christians. Kilian lived long enough to participate in Bernard's wedding – just two days before his death.[3]

Hermann, the youngest son, was only twenty-four and still single. Just the previous year he had been installed as the pastor and succeeded his father. The father, early in Hermann's life, had identified academic ability in Hermann and hoped he would become a pastor. After confirmation, the father began teaching Hermann Latin so that he would be prepared to attend the synodical *Gymnasium* at Fort Wayne, Indiana. He, like his brother Gerhard, left home to attend school in the North when he was only fourteen. His mother and sisters shed tears when he left for the journey, but he was escorted by his experienced brother Gerhard. The program of study at Fort Wayne was designed to prepare the students for the ministry and lasted six years, four of high school and two of college. They were not easy years for either Hermann or his father. Because of the distance frequent journeys to Texas were not financially feasible and he spent his first summer vacation at Fort Wayne. Correspondence was the only form of communication, and the father wrote frequently to both his son and the school administrators. The separation from the family at such an early age required the father's wisdom on such matters as the use of tobacco, finances, and scholarship. But he eventually completed his preparation at Fort Wayne and then, in 1883, his theological studies at Concordia Seminary at St. Louis.[4]

And finally there was the youngest, Hulda, twenty-three and also single. She became her mother's support when Theresia left home; and, when her mother died, she became the woman of the house and attended to her father and brothers. She was cheerful and spritely and had developed skills in knitting and crocheting. The fact that she married a pastor from a neighboring parish several years later, would have delighted her father.

Kilian's children had been his primary concern. Even when they were still young, he thought ahead about their education. Opportunities for advanced education were limited in Texas and at one time he even considered returning to Europe to facilitate their schooling. Although the educational question was settled for the boys, by their being sent away from home at an early age, he also worried about the future of all his children, especially that of the girls, in "half-wild Texas." He also contemplated taking a parish in the North to help his children achieve a higher status and avoid a life living in the shabby condition of the Serbin farmers and businessmen. But he stayed in Texas and learned to accept their choices.[5]

After the service in church ended, the mourners followed the crucifer, carrying the black processional cross with a silver corpus, and the casket to the adjoining cemetery. The stone church and cemetery were situated on ninety-five acres the congregation owned. Other buildings on that land included the parsonage, two of its rooms standing much as they had been when built in 1855; the old frame church building, dedicated on Christmas Day, 1859, serving as the school and Gerhard's residence; and the barn, sheds and a concrete-lined cistern. About one-fourth mile away, on the other side of the cemetery, was another church constructed of wood, called St. Peter's church. The pastor of that church was Pastor Geyer, who preached at the funeral. The congregation was not as large as St. Paul's, but it also had a school. The cemetery, where the members of the congregation said farewell to their venerable pastor, was shared by the two congregations. In the cemetery, where the late pastor would join

Processional cross
Source: Jack Wiederhold

his wife, already lay their first daughter, Maria Theresia, born two months after the voyage to Texas and the first person to be interred in the new cemetery.[6]

Even though the funeral followed a usual pattern of funerals and the daily lives of the parishioner had become routine, their lives and the life of their pastor had been anything but routine. Forty-three of Kilian's seventy-three years had been spent in Europe. There his career lasted twenty years while in Texas it reached twenty-nine years. It was almost as if he had lived two separate lives – each career, even though both were in the ministry, was most unlike the other. His life, just as theirs, had been full of visions and goals, conflict and tragedy, success and failure. What would life have been for the listeners if Kilian had stayed in Europe? Would they have stayed? Had he made the right choices?

TEXAS

Texas, in 1854, had survived its revolution for independence, the ten years as a republic, and economic indebtedness. When Kilian reached Texas in that year, Texas had been a state in the United States for eight years and although statehood brought greater stability, Texas was a frontier area. Governor Elisha Pease identified three state issues that needed attention: the establishment of a public school system, improvement of the system of transportation, and the Indians living in the state. It was the land of a second chance for many people both from United States and Europe, and Kilian and the Wends were only a small part of the large number of immigrants who wanted to start again.

The *Ben Nevis* arrived at Galveston Island on December 14. Cholera no longer claimed lives and in the calm weather Kilian conducted a service and evening devotions. The next morning the captain went to Galveston in a small boat and made arrangements for a steamer to ferry the passengers and their belongings to land. Then, finally, on December 16, they entered Galveston and Kilian took his family to a hotel to rest while the remaining passengers and baggage could be brought in.

After paying a few dollars duty, the immigrants boarded steamers for the final leg of their sea journey. There in Houston the group stayed for a week until every one arrived and until preparations for land travel could be made. The Kilians stayed with the Lutheran pastor, Caspar Braun, and, together with his congregation, celebrated their first Christmas in their new homeland.[7]

For their journey into the interior, the Kilians and five other families hired two wagons, each drawn by ten oxen to transport their belongings the eigthy-five miles to New Ulm. Everyone except the children and the pregnant Mrs. Kilian walked across the soggy, wet prairie. In the evenings they used their bedspreads as tents and slept under their feather beds. When they reached the Brazos River, it was in flood stage, so rather than spend the night on the wet ground, Kilian took his family to an inn. But the inn was filled so the three sat out the night in a shed with a leaky roof. After fifteen days, they arrived at New Ulm.

When they arrived at New Ulm, however, the cabins and farm lots were overflowing with other Wends, so the Kilians traveled yet another forty miles to the house of a Wendish family living on Rabbs Creek. There was some urgency because Mrs. Kilian was approaching the time of childbirth. And on February 13, Maria Theresia was born and baptized. One month later she died.[8]

KILIAN AND THE PREVIOUS EMIGRANTS

Two sets of Wends had preceded Kilian and the congregation to Texas and they presented opposite responses to the new arrivals. The first and smaller group was represented by the Helas, Seydler, and Wagner families who had migrated between 1849 and 1851. Although they were Wends and were from Bautzen, their motives for migration are not known; they were part of the broader German migration. They had settled near New Ulm, a large German settlement in Austin County and High Hill in Fayette County. While they aided the new immigrants, they sent letters back to Bautzen in which they leveled harsh criticism against Kilian and, to some extent, against the lay leaders. These letters were published in the Wendish newspaper before Kilian could respond, but the editor did send Kilian a copy so Kilian could defend himself.

The first charge was against the dream of building a new colony. They pointed out that the days of land grants from the state of Texas had ended for those who entered Texas after 1853. Land in the settled areas that was suitable for a colony had become too expensive and the living costs during the first year were beyond the means of the group.

Land on the frontier was cheaper, but there the Indians were a threat and no protection was available against raids. Even the league of land which some leaders had just bought was overgrown and wooded and not suitable for good farms. In Europe small plots might be adequate for subsistence, but in Texas owning large blocks of land was a necessity. They had advised the newcomers against the attempt to found a colony, and predicted a failure for the venture. As evidence, they called attention to the ongoing dispersion of settlers from the main group even though a block of land had been purchased. The first charge was defensible. These early emigrants knew Texas and could see the unrealistic dream of a colony. A community perhaps, but not a colony.

The second charge the old settlers raised was mismanagement and exploitation of the followers by Kilian and the leaders. This charge was unfair and based on hindsight. They argued that the *Ben Nevis* passengers paid $55 for each passenger instead of $50 for any other ships, and that they had been warned against going through England. While some of the details were true, the entire immigrant group had decided to stay together and travel on a single ship, and that ship was available in England, not Hamburg. Those who could pay were required to contribute to a treasury which paid for the passages of the poor. But that decision also had been made in Europe so that everyone could be included.[9]

Certainly the Wends had scattered and were looking for food, shelter and employment; and under those conditions dissatisfaction would arise. In all likelihood that dissatisfaction was communicated to the earlier settlers and they sent letters back to Bautzen. These letters were of great irritation to Kilian because they were not only unfair and published before he was given a chance to respond, but they could be used by those who opposed his migration and who hoped to hinder further departures for America. Kilian was not oblivious to this opposition and heard that harsh letters were on their way. On March 19, 1855, he wrote to Teacher Dutschmann in Weigersdorf that he had written to friends for copies so he could respond. Included on a list of friends was the editor, Jan Smoler, but Smoler published the letters before sending Kilian copies.[10] Kilian did not forget and for years there was an estrangement between Kilian and Smoler, two Wends who supported the Wendish cause.

The response of the second group of Wends was quite the opposite. They had migrated in 1853 and had also found homes in the German communities of Austin County. It was a larger group than the critics and was composed of thirty-five who had separated themselves from the Prussian church and had been members of the Weigersdorf congregation. Upon their arrival in Houston, they had located one of the Seydler brothers who worked there as a mason and obtained directions for New Ulm.

Their favorable letters home, in turn, influenced the Weigersdorf and Klitten Wends who had been contemplating a voyage to Australia. The *Ben Nevis* migrants were relatives, friends and neighbors, and they were welcomed with open arms. One of these settlers, August Polnick, provided shelter for Kilian while the leaders were looking for a block of land. Some of these 1853 migrants eventually moved to Serbin; and during the interim, Kilian traveled every six weeks to New Ulm to minister to them.[11]

ESTABLISHING SERBIN

While Kilian and his family remained with the Polnicks, the lay leaders searched for a suitable block of land which they could purchase. Vacant land was available, but all too often the owner could not be located. Finally, on February 11, 1855, Carl Lehmann found an owner who was willing to sell. As the transfer of title was not completed until mid-March the immigrants were forced to continue living in their encampment and hence lost precious time for the preparation of fields for planting.[12]

Those were months of instability for Kilian as well. While everyone else was working on construction of their own homes and fields, a shelter for Kilian's small family had to wait, and they found shelter with other families. Finally, on October 14, 1855 he believed that he had waited long enough and presented the congregation with a list of promises they had made and not honored. He asked for the compensation they agreed to pay him for the first year and for greater efforts on the building that would serve as the church, school and his home. In addition there was a need for a smoke house, a pig pen, and plowing some land set aside for a garden and field. He reminded them that they had promised to support him for one year and that if they could not renew the agreement, he was willing to resume negotiations with the Australian Wends and serve them.

The ultimatum stimulated the members to action and three days later the Kilians moved into a cabin of two rooms that would serve as home until his death in 1884. One of the rooms doubled as a church until 1859 and as a school until 1871. In 1857 a veranda and a second wing for use as a kitchen were added. At the end of the wing they built a shelter for the church bell and began using it at Pentecost.[13]

KILIAN AS PASTOR

The call which Kilian accepted in 1854 provided a job description for him. As the pastor he was expected to perform the office of the ministry and administer the sacraments "according to the Lutheran religious custom." While that Lutheran custom was not specifically spelled out, there must have been a consensus on its meaning and it was most likely used to stand in contrast to the Calvinist practices. The practice further took for granted not only sermons on Sunday in Wendish, but also church services on the two days after major church festivals, such as Christmas and Easter. Besides preaching and administering the sacraments of Baptism and the Lord's Supper, there were many little acts that were identified because they included an assessment which would be granted to Kilian.

That list, for example, included recognition of a mother at her first church attendance after childbirth. In the event of a marriage, he made the preliminary announcements of the wedding, performed the ceremony, and assisted if one of the partners was from a different congregation. At a funeral ceremony he preached a funeral sermon and delivered an obituary. He would also hear confessions, instruct children for confirmation, provide church certificates for baptism, marriages, and deaths and record these events into the church records.

He was also expected to teach the children for the entire year. There was no school on festival days or during the time when children were needed in the fields, such as August when cotton was picked.

The subject matter included both religious and secular material and was in Wendish and German.

Other duties he assumed as the need arose included a church service in German as well as Bible classes on Sunday afternoon and on holiday afternoons. And for some time, because not all of the group settled in Serbin, he made the fifty mile trip on horseback to New Ulm every fifth week.

In return for his services he was promised 1,000 Taler for the first year, small fees or perquisites for officiating at weddings, funerals, and other church functions, a parsonage, and land for a garden and animals. Especially in the early years during the settling-in period and the drought years, the promises were not met.

Although his call expired after the first year, no efforts were made to issue a call for a second year or for a permanent call. Included in the October 1855 document listing his desires was a reminder of a call. He fully sympathized with the members' desire to meet their necessities, but his office in the congregation could no longer be ignored. Realizing that the existence of the congregation was still tenuous, he expressed his willingness to accept a second call limited to one year.

During the first year, Kilian bought a cow and horse for $50 each, and in time he purchased some land for himself and for his family in the event of his death. In the Census of 1860, the first census to list the Wends, Kilian was listed as a farmer, not as a clergyman. Kilian reported that he owned twenty acres of improved land and thirty unimproved acres with an estimated value of $200. His livestock, including two milk cows and thirty range cattle, was valued at $240. On his twenty acres he produced ten bushels of rye, one-hundred bushels of Indian corn, and one bale of cotton. The fact that his machinery and implements were valued at only $5.00 suggests that the members of the congregation did his plowing and harrowing. By 1870 Kilian's role was more clearly identified and he was not listed in the agricultural census. But he estimated the value of his personal property and land at about $3,000. Four years later, the Panic of 1873 drew the United States into a depression and Kilian's estate lost some of its value.

In addition to his occupation as pastor, his role as teacher, his work in the fields, and tending his garden, Kilian also served as a homeopathic doctor. He brought a collection of medicines with him from Europe and, although we do not know the extent of his practice, he attended to people, even some who severed connections with his church.[14]

KILIAN AND RELIGIOUS AFFILIATION

When Kilian and his congregation left Europe, they also severed religious ties and associations. In Texas, they could either remain independent of any affiliations, join an existing association, or create a new one. Kilian's ministry had never been one of isolation from other pastors but one of allegiance with other organizations. As pastor in Kotitz he was part of the Saxon state church. Even when he became the pastor of the independent congregations of Weigersdorf and Klitten, he affiliated with the Old Lutherans of Silesia.[15] Religious isolation was not part of his tradition.

Upon his arrival in Houston in December 1854 Kilian formed a friendship with Caspar Braun, a pastor who had migrated to Texas in 1850. Braun's theological training was not as extensive as Kilian's and may have been limited to five weeks at St. Chrischona mission school in Basel, the same institution Kilian visited when he was contemplating overseas missions. Braun had migrated to Pennsylvania in 1847 and was admitted to the Pittsburgh Synod. He served several small congregations, but after some difficulties he resigned and traveled to Texas. Kilian spent his first Christmas in Texas with Braun and their friendship endured for their lifetime. There may have been religious differences, but if there were, they seemed to tolerate each other's position and overlook those differences.[16]

Braun had been the host pastor for the group that formed the First Evangelical Lutheran Synod in Texas and served as its first president. This synod, known as the Texas Synod, could have certified Kilian, but Kilian was hesitant because he spotted too many similarities with the Prussian Union which he left, and he also bemoaned a lack of liturgy which he believed enriched the church service.

Instead Kilian was drawn to the Missouri Synod or the full title, The German Evangelical Lutheran Synod of Missouri, Ohio and Other States, an association of congregations and pastors that had been formed in 1847.[17] The president of the organization and the editor of *Der Lutheraner*, the official organ, was C. F. W. Walther. Kilian and Walther had both graduated from the same school of theology at the University of Leipzig. Some writers emphasize the friendship between Kilian and Walther and attribute Kilian's decision to join the Missouri Synod to that friendship. Making a decision of such significance because of friendship would have been out of character for Kilian, and in a letter introducing himself to Walther he gave no indication of friendship or even being acquainted. Walther began study at the seminary in 1829 while Kilian began in 1831, and during Kilian's first year, Walther did not attend because of his health. Walther returned to the university in 1832 for his last year while Kilian was in his second year. During that time they could have become acquainted. But when introducing himself to Walther, Kilian provides the name of Dr. Wilhelm Sihler, another founder of the Synod, as a reference. "My request for authorization from your synod is based on my personal acquaintance with Dr. Sihler." Sihler had visited Kilian at Kotitz prior to Sihler's departure to America.[18]

Kilian knew of Walther through Walther's writings and agreed with the polity of the synod which empowered the voters' assembly as the supreme authority and diminished the power of the ecclesiastical leaders such as the pastor and bishop. Kilian owned a copy of *Stimme der Kirche in der Frage von Kirche und Amt,* written by Walther, and published in Erlangen in 1852, in which these views are articulated. Kilian also preferred the Missouri Synod to the General Synod which was an umbrella group for many Lutherans in the eastern United States, and a group the founders of the Missouri Synod found objectionable.

The precipitating factor in Kilian's decision to seek some sort of affiliation was the requirement of the state of Texas on matters such as officiating at marriages. In Germany the role of the pastor as a functionary of the government was extensive, while in Texas, where the churches were independent, the state regulated only those religious acts that had a civil dimension. For Texas to recognize the legal status of religious marriages, the pastor was required to be a member of a denomination. The matter was vital in Serbin because husbands lost their wives and wives lost their husbands to cholera and marriages of widows and widowers were an immediate concern. If Kilian were not authorized, the service would be carried out in another church or by a justice of the peace in a secular ceremony.[19] Kilian could choose between the association in Texas which was nearby but with whom he disagreed, or the St. Louis association which was distant but with whom he agreed. He chose the Missouri Synod and became the first Missouri Synod pastor in Texas. His congregation remained independent until 1866 when it also affiliated with the Missouri Synod.

By joining the Missouri Synod, Kilian gained his certification and became a member of a denomination, but Kilian did not solve his personal isolation because there would be no other pastors of the Missouri Synod in the state until 1868. His communication with colleagues could only be in written form, although in 1860 he traveled to St. Louis to attend the synodical meeting. "It is painful to be here all alone," he said, and in 1858 Kilian even considered forming another association of Lutherans in Texas.[20]

The Civil War intensified his isolation when communication with St. Louis was interrupted and when the Union blockade disrupted communication with Europe. Letters to Europe were first sent to Mexico and returning letters needed to be addressed to Matamoros, Mexico. Kilian resigned himself to reading synodical publications, which provided "joy in my loneliness."

Even after the Civil War the feeling of personal isolation continued and he expressed his joy to Director T. C. W. Lindemann of the Addison Seminary that in Lindemann he had found "a friend and correspondent, someone I have been searching for as long as I have been in America." Kilian complained that his European friends seldom responded, and if they did they doubted Kilian's statements. Even Walther he found reserved, although friendly. In Lindemann, Kilian "found a friend who comforts me in my problems."[21]

Membership in a synod also provided other services. One service that Kilian would find beneficial was the training of pastors and teachers and the placement of these individuals into congregations.

Kilian ardently supported these institutions and collected money for them at weddings and baptisms. His sons would attend these institutions and his congregation would obtain personnel through the synod. The Synod also provided assistance in conflict resolution through a system known as a visitation. In the event of a conflict in a congregation, whether between factions within the congregation, between pastor and laity, or even doctrinal issues, a neutral party in the form of a visitor could examine the problem. The visitor could be an elected official such as a district president or a parish pastor appointed to represent the synod. There would be several visitations during Kilian's ministry, officially on a four-year cycle, and the visitors traveled either from St. Louis or from New Orleans.

CONVENTICLES (*STUNDENCHRISTEN*)

The seeds of division in the Serbin congregation were sown even before the group left Europe. The majority of the immigrant group originated from Prussia and had left the state church to form an independent congregation. However, approximately two-hundred Saxons living near the Prussian border remained within their state church but had adopted the conventicles as their religious safety-valve. In Europe the people of the conventicle movement had supported Kilian, but in Texas the meetings became the hotbed of opposition. The Saxons criticized Prussians for their withdrawal from the State church, and Kilian and the Prussians faulted the Saxons for their insistence on prayer meetings as sign of a living faith. Both segments agreed on the essential, however, and that basis was the Lutheran Confessions.[22]

While Kilian grouped the Saxons and the *Stundenchristen* in one camp and the Prussians and himself in the other, the lines were not that clearly drawn. Some Prussians, such as Polnick, supported the conventicles and many Saxons favored a liturgical service. Even so, the Saxons who joined the emigration organization had not been in his independent congregation and did not possess that personal loyalty toward Kilian, nor had they experienced the struggle of leaving a state church.

There was no evidence of discord on this issue during the journey, but in 1857 the controversy surfaced in the congregation during the formulation of a congregational constitution and policies regarding the spiritual life of the members. The conventicleists asked for a devotional format and firm application of church discipline, while the opponents favored a formal church service and argued that such discipline would not result in better, more Christian, lives.

Just when this controversy was escalating, the German Methodists led by the Rev. E. Schneider began holding camp meetings at a place approximately four miles from Serbin and invited neighboring Wends to the meetings. They first converted some Germans from the Moravian Brethren tradition who had been worshiping with Kilian. And then Widow Teschke, who had married Johann Noack, a Wend, attended one of the meetings and she was so overtaken by the spirit of laughing and ecstasy that she wanted to ascend into heaven. Other conventicle proponents attended as well.

Kilian responded with a sermon and reminded his listeners of the Calvinism in Prussia and that Methodism was another form of that same Calvinism but through the English tradition. He admonished them for attending revivals and instead encouraged them to examine the public confession of a church. If they were attending the revivals simply because there were revivals, what would happen if different denominations sponsored other revivals? Would they chase from one denomination to another? Kilian, under pressure, proposed prayer meetings, everyone invited, every Wednesday and Friday night. He provided a text and a short introduction and encouraged discussion. The opening and closing prayers were spoken as the participants kneeled and for the closing prayer Kilian asked a layman he could trust to lead a prayer. The Methodist threat was repulsed and the only Wendish losses were Johann Noack and his wife.

Kilian even conceded that some good resulted from the meetings and that they had "cleaned the Lutheran fountains." Attendance sagged, however, because of inclement weather and especially during a study of the unemotional Augsburg Confession, so Kilian ended the sessions at Easter 1858, six months after they had started. The

Stundenchristen blamed the declining interest with Kilian's prayer meetings on his choice of topics and the rigid structure of the meetings. So when the Methodists resumed their preaching, the conventicle people again associated with them. Kilian, sensing a growing division in the congregation, on the Sunday before Pentecost, stated that three options existed. Either there would be a reconciliation, or a division, or his departure. The date for a congregational meeting was set and the conventicleists were encouraged to attend.[23]

Instead, on May 25, 1858 they sent Kilian a letter proposing a separation. In contrast to Kilian and his supporters, they believed that faith and life were one and "by their fruit ye shall know them." They believed that there could be no resolution. The leaders were August Polnick from Weigersdorf, Michael Urban from Kubschütz, Andreas Hantschke (Prochneschko) from Baruth, Johann Urban, from Rackel, Matteas Schmidt (Hunter-Schmidt) from Reichwalde, Matheas Wagner from Halbendorf, Jacob Moerbe, (Neudorf), Ernst Moerbe (Klix), Johann Lorentschk (Reichwalde), August Dube (Rodewitz), Johannn Zenich, [Schönig](Baruth), Christoph Kokel, (Reichwalde), and Jacob Urban (Kubschutz).[24]

Kilian responded with a letter signed by the church council and his supporters and confronted the dissenters with a charge of joining with the Methodists and for acting in a self-righteous manner. "That exactly is your transgression that you consort with the enemy and 'the little flock' looks at 'the large group' with a pharisaical eye. That is the fruit by which we know you." Even after such strong language the letter requested further discussion and unity.

Kilian's attempt to get to the center of the conventicle controversy was a short essay on the "The Certainty of Salvation," which he sent to Gumlich and requested the church in Prussia for an opinion. Kilian proposed that there were two types of certainty: the ordinary and the extraordinary. The ordinary is found in Scripture in such places as the Beatitudes in Matthew 5, while the extraordinary certainty takes place through revelations, visions, and exuberant feelings. Ordinary certainty is all that is needed, while the extraordinary, though noticeable, cannot be demanded from everyone and even carries some dangers with it. How can one be sure that the responses resulting from fire and brimstone sermons, exhilarating songs, and emotional prayers are indeed true and valid? Are the sources of the visions from God or from the devil? And even if the responses are assumed to be from God, do they not bring about arrogance on the part of the recipient and division in the congregation?

The final attempt at reconciliation was made on October 10, 1858, but the meeting deteriorated into further recrimination. Kilian's sermons with his focus on the Gospel, the minority charged, had no power. Preaching the law in all its severity was needed to bring repentance. That repentance and faith transcended all denominational boundaries, and man-made bodies were not important. So a split followed on October 16, 1858, with the creation of another Lutheran congregation which was called St. Peter's. Kilian noted that these people, even though they liked the emotionalism of the Methodists, could not accept the Calvinist views of the Lord's Supper.

During the controversy both the dissidents and Kilian had sent letters to Dr. Walther. Walther, after some delay, took Kilian's side so in 1860 St. Peter's joined the Texas Synod. St. Peter's had built a frame church, but the congregation did not prosper and never exceeded forty-five communicants. Kilian's congregation, on the other hand, was not severely damaged. Immigrants moved into the community to make up for those numbers lost, and the need for a church building was obvious. The Voters' Assembly passed around a subscription list. Enough people pledged $5.00 so the cornerstone was laid on November 11, 1859. Using volunteer labor, the building, measuring 50 x 25 x 14, was completed by the next Christmas and so was an addition on the parsonage.[25]

Reunion of the two congregations may have happened sooner had it not been for a Wendish pastor, Gottfried Lehnigk. Earlier Kilian had written to Lusatia asking for a successor to the Serbin pulpit in case he would return to Europe. The pastor of Kilian's former parish at Weigersdorf informed Kilian about Lehnigk. Lehnigk, a Wend, who had been a member of the Old Lutheran congregation at Döbrick, near Cottbus, had migrated to the United States in 1864 and was studying at the St. Louis Seminary. When the Civil War ended, Kilian corresponded with the officials and learned that Lehnigk had graduated from the practical seminary, then located in St. Louis. After his graduation he had been ordained and installed at California City, Missouri. Early in 1866, however, Lehnigk had resigned because of ill health.

With the information about Lehnigk, Kilian encouraged the congregation to affiliate with the Missouri Synod. Even though Kilian had joined the Synod earlier, congregational membership was a separate matter. Kilian reasoned that congregational membership in the synod would contribute toward the resolution of the division in the congregation. In addition, synodical membership would enable the congregation to obtain orthodox pastors and teachers from the synodical institutions and to call pastors, such as Lehnigk, from synodical congregations. The Voters' Assembly passed the resolution on December 17, 1865, and after some negotiations, the membership became official in 1866.

Kilian corresponded with Lehnigk, and he arrived at Serbin in July 1866. Kilian invited him into his home and provided him with room and board. After a period of serious illness, Lehnigk recovered and early in 1867 took over the school for Kilian.

Just as St. Peter's congregation was on the brink of returning, Lehnigk, injected himself into the scene and took the side of the pietistic group. He maintained that Kilian was too lenient and he hoped to use the controversy to establish a model Missouri congregation with strict church discipline and confessional adherence. Eventually both Kilian and Lehnigk wrote letters of complaint to St. Louis about each other, even though they remained on good terms and Lehnigk continued to live in Kilian's house. The President of the Western District, C. T. H. Fick responded to Kilian that he would visit Serbin but that he could not condemn Lehnigk's actions. Kilian was incensed not only because Lehnigk and Fick were acquainted, but because St Paul congregation had affiliated with the Missouri Synod and St. Peter had not. How could the Synod treat its own members so? "I feel betrayed and sold."[26]

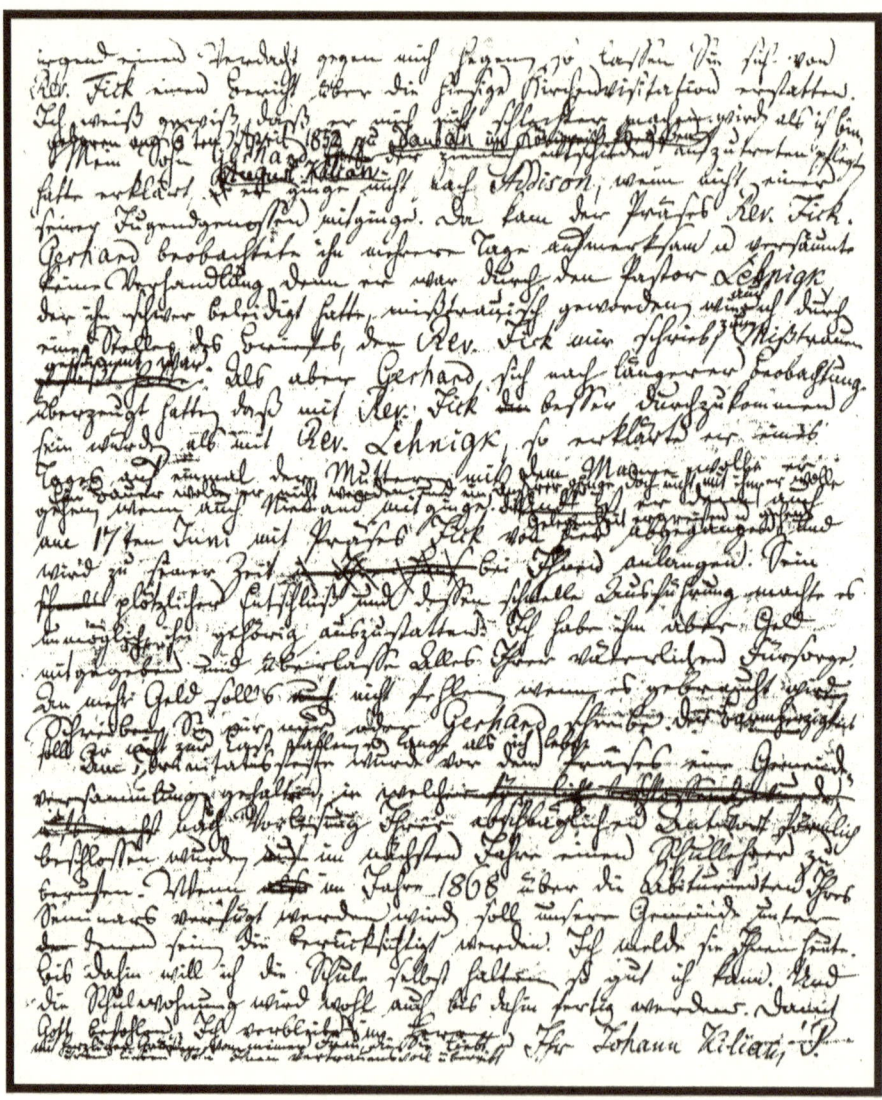

Example of Kilian's draft of a letter
Source: Concordia Historical Institute

Kilian, did not passively sit back and grumble. He wrote directly to Walther and clearly stated that his congregation would withdraw from Synod if Synod took St. Peter's side and Lehnigk became the pastor of that congregation. And given the fact that Lehnigk "was an indefatigable debater and indestructible quarreler [but] usually sick from distress and anxiety when he must preach," St. Peter congregation would fail. Lehnigk would probably marry and leave the congregation just as the previous Texas Synod pastors and done, and then there would be no Missouri Synod congregation in Texas. "I would certainly stand, for I am like a tree that stands alone in the field, but securely anchored with roots and displaying extensive gnarled branches..., but I fear that without this warning the dear Missouri Synod can cover itself with shame in Texas."

Kilian must have made his point. When Lehnigk attended the denomination's Western District convention in Chicago, he was told not to return to Serbin. Shortly thereafter, from Frohna, Missouri, he sent a letter of apology to Kilian and the congregation; and although Kilian could not understand his actions, he counted him as a friend. At Pentecost, 1867 Fick, representing the Synod, traveled from Collinsville, Illinois, vindicated Kilian and reconciled the two congregations. Kilian entrusted Fick with his eldest son who would become a student at the fledgling synodical institution for training teachers at Addison, Illinois.[27]

KILIAN'S TWO PILLARS

Close and detailed descriptions of quarrels and controversies could well sully the good and positive elements in the life of any person or group and seem to have little value when that issue no longer resonates in contemporary times. Nevertheless, analyzing controversies is important even if doing so appears to be excessive negativism because it helps identify those issues which a person considers vital and worthy of unpleasantness. Most people are not argumentative and eager to confront others, write extensive letters, or make enemies. Yet controversies show which issues a person holds paramount and for which he is willing to give up peace for turmoil.

And so the conventicle controversy tells us about Kilian and his principles.

Second Serbin church and school
Source: Texas Wendish Heritage Society

Kilian believed that a Lutheran congregation should be the center of community life and conventicles distracted from the focus of the church. For that principle he was willing to expend his energies and in the middle of the conventicle controversy, on Christmas Day in1860, Kilian expanded on his principle. The occasion was the dedication of the new church that had been more than thirteen months in construction. For almost six years the congregation had gathered in one of the two rooms of the parsonage that during the week also served as the school, and a larger facility was overdue. The congregation members agreed to the construction of a separate church building using their own labor, but inactivity was more evident than participation and Kilian complained about the lack of progress. The conventicle controversy had drained the enthusiasm from what should have been an invigorating project. But when the conventicleists departed and constructed a separate church which they called St.

Peter, Kilian's larger group speeded the completion of its own building.

As part of the dedication, Kilian prepared a statement in English for those people of the community who were not part of the congregation. Even though the statement reflects reliance on a dictionary, one can envy Kilian's ability in learning a foreign language in five years while dealing with Wendish and German on a daily basis. The statement, filled with platitudes for America, was much more than a gracious welcome to the visitors. Kilian spoke of the foundation of his faith and the purpose of the congregation. He also artfully juxtaposed the commonly accepted negative references of the old world (Catholic and Masonic) with his opponents in the new (conventicles) and then followed with his mission statement.

> Now we commit to God's free grace and efficiency [power], how he may work in the hearts of men by his word and by his Sacraments. We want no magnificence of dominion, no succession of the bishops, no radiance of the clergy, no auricular confession, no secret orders, no pious fraternities, no monasteries, no private conventicles, no intercession of the deceased saints, no letters of indulgence, no pilgrimages, no camp meetings, no ecstasies, no noise, no artificial excitation nor any like invention of man, we want only the Word and Sacraments pure and unmixed according to the commandments of Christ, numerous assemblies of attentive and sacramentally united hearers, on the Sundays and holy days, a decent and pleasing meeting-house and a becoming behaviour of the whole congregation, that we may enlarge the blessings of this country and that our posterity may continue in the christian faith. That's our intention, that's our desire, that's our endeavour....

Kilian described a Lutheran community, not based on good works, but based on grace available through the Word and Sacraments. That was Luther's teaching and it was Kilian's first guiding principle. That principle had been the goal in Europe and the conventicleists had threatened its existence in America with their emphasis on good works. His opposition to the United Church in Prussia and to the Texas Synod symbolized his fear that Lutheranism was being eroded, but purity must be maintained in the new Wendish congregation in Serbin by adherence to the doctrines expressed in the confessions and creeds.[28]

The second principle was the Wendish language, and a later controversy would highlight it. Kilian wanted to preserve a Wendish congregation, and the threat from German would come later and with it the second schism. Interestingly, Kilian addressed the visitors to the church dedication in English, yet he did not consider those who spoke English as mission prospects, nor did he provide a church service for them. He had made an eloquent statement of faith in English, but his mission was not to the English. His mission was to the Wends and incidentally to the Germans. One can only speculate how Serbin would have been different if the Wends had made the transition to English as their second language, rather than German.

These two pillars had supported Kilian's philosophy already in Europe, and among all the hymns he had translated or created, the one that appealed to him and his people the most was the one that always returned to the refrain: "Wends, to your faith and to your language remain true."[29]

KILIAN'S RELATION WITH EUROPEANS

Kilian's very act of migration cost him the friendship of some people in Europe. One group critical of his action was composed of fellow Lutherans. The loss of three-hundred Prussian Lutherans and a pastor weakened the Old Lutheran movement against the United Church even though the loss was only one-sixth of the congregation and the property which was sold was purchased by the Lutherans who remained. Kilian, however, was the only Sorb pastor in the Lutheran church in Prussia and finding a replacement who could handle the Sorbian language was a necessity, but would also be difficult. And, of course, the greater the number who followed, the weaker the movement would be.[30]

When the conventicle controversy developed, Kilian worried about his reputation and worked hard at maintaining the relationship with the Lutherans. Most difficult to win to his side was the segment of Lutherans who were inclined toward pietism. They would be more sympathetic with the conventicleists and they would be easily alienated. They tended to believe the letters from Texas which found fault with Kilian and undermined his reputation. Kilian was almost obsessed with telling his side of the controversy no matter which way they leaned.

His most faithful correspondent in the early days was Pastor Gotthold Albert Gumlich, who succeeded him at Weigersdorf. He asked Gumlich to collect and send him letters that attempted to discredit him. Kilian promised that this "defamation of character will be answered in a letter by the remaining portion of my faithful congregation." The congregation did not respond, but Kilian did so with detailed descriptions of the controversy and with a statement he had written about the topic itself. He also authorized Gumlich to publish some of the information in church publications such as the *Kirchenblatt*, the journal of the Old Lutherans.

Any requests for clarification or questions from his friends irritated Kilian, and any indication of doubt from his friends led him to write strident letters. To Pastor Gumlich he wrote that he expected complete impartiality until Kilian's side could be presented and hoped that the earlier displeasure over Kilian's migration would not make him susceptible to believing false accusations. Kilian defended American freedom of religion against Gumlich's suggestion that there were inadequate controls in America and said, "I believe that it is good when all religious tendencies, good and bad ones, unfold themselves fully and unhindered, so that all can see to where they lead." He also defended the Missouri Synod that was taking his side. "The brethren in the North know me better, than you know me, the way I see it now. Otherwise you would not believe that my gifts will fall into decay unused and that I am in great danger of becoming a Texas cattle-breeder or farmer."[31]

While most of Kilian's letters and documents focused on the conventicle controversy, he also responded to a charge of drunkenness. There was no truth to the charge, but the response is instructive as to the level of the ill will generated by the conventicle controversy as well as the hardship Kilian endured as he ministered to his distant members. The charge had never been raised in Serbin, where it would have been ridiculed, but only in a letter to Lusatia to a receptive audience. The incident took place in early January 1857, when Kilian traveled to New Ulm to conduct services. While he was there, a north wind swept in and blew so hard that only the nearest neighbors could attend. Kilian spent the next day in New Ulm in the hope that the winds would abate. They did not, and he could wait no longer because he needed to be in Serbin for Sunday services. Part of his preparation for heading into a wind-driven rain included a practice he had learned two years earlier from the drivers who hauled his freight from Houston to the interior. "Naturally, I also took the usual protective substance against the cold and freezing – whiskey, which over here is the customary rather strong drink, to keep me warm. This preservative is so much more necessary in Texas because here as soon as a person begins to freeze inwardly from the wetness and cold, fever follows." In spite of the whiskey and warm clothes, riding the horse in the blustery wind was such misery that he dismounted and led the horse. At one point, nearing exhaustion, he slipped and muddied his clothes. He took shelter at the Scharaths where his clothes were washed. He neither fell from his horse nor did he vomit from too much whiskey as was charged. "Incidentally," he added, crediting his regimen, "I have been healthy for four years in spite of much illness which has prevailed among our people in past years."

The letters and documents had varied results. Some Europeans such as Gumlich and Kubitz supported Kilian, others opposed him, and still others believed that they were "all sick." For Kilian the correspondence had been time-consuming and frustrating, and quite possibly after he had spent five years in Texas, his emotional dependence on Europe was diminishing. So in 1859 he apologized to Gumlich that his letters might have been hurtful and asked for an armistice of two years. "Then the present fogs will have lifted and your side will also be able to see clearer than you see now." Kilian also anticipated conflict with the Missouri Synod over millennialism that would demand his attention. "Therefore I must withdraw my troops from Weigersdorf" so he would not be overextended.[32]

Several years later when Kilian wrote to the church officials in Saxony, inquiring about openings in Sorbian congregations, there was very little interest in his services. Perhaps Kilian's confrontational approach overshadowed his struggle to defend his reputation.

The other European group, the Wendish nationalist movement, also saw the migration damaging the cause because it weakened resistance to Germanization. Kilian had been influential in the preservation of the language and was also a member of the *Maćic Serbski* and the Upper Lusatian Association of Knowledge in Görlitz. There had been friction before because Kilian maintained that Sorbian nationality and Lutheran faith were inseparable. The Sorbian intelligensia, on the other hand, believed that faith had to be subordinated to nationality. Nationality was the single goal and confessional elements weakened the cause of Sorbian secular interests. Kilian and the prominent Sorbs were united in the cause for Sorbs but divided on religious emphasis.

A leading nationalist and editor of the Sorbian newspaper, Jan Smoler, did not give Kilian favored treatment and printed the critical letters. Kilian had cut out the critical letters printed in the *Serbske Nowiny* in 1855 and kept them for himself. Only later in 1859 did he show them to Carl Lehmann. Kilian concluded that Smoler was an enemy and discouraged subscriptions to his Wendish newspaper. Even in 1859 when a false rumor was spread that Kilian was interested in returning to Lusatia, Kilian would not write to Smoler directly, but asked Lehman to write for him.

In 1868 Kilian himself wrote to Smoler and laid the basis for a renewed friendship. Kilian wrote: "You know, at the outset, that you were not favorably inclined towards me when I emigrated from Sorbia, and that just because I emigrated." Smoler printed the letter in the newspaper and inserted his comment: "Later this antipathy disappeared altogether, as could be noticed, that even though you had emigrated you remained faithful to those who accompanied you." Finally in 1872 Kilian further mended his fences with Smoler and subscribed to the *Serbske Nowiny*, and closed with "God go with you. I remain affectionately your humble Johann Kilian P[astor]." [33]

The extent of Kilian's alienation from the Wendish intellectuals was demonstrated when a Wendish dictionary by Ch. Tr. Pfuhl was published in 1866. While a dictionary may be viewed as nothing more than a book for checking spelling and definitions, it is a symbol of nationalism as well. It shows that the language is respected and helps consolidate the people who use it. Kilian was not even informed about its existence until 1872 and was miffed. "I find it odd that I first learned of this dictionary and that no one informed me of such a noteworthy appearance of things Sorbian. My old friend Imiš, Wanak and others appear to have assumed that I had become lost in my Texas oak forest, or even have died. Otherwise they surely would have written."

He then proceeded to write the author, Dr. Pfuhl, a long letter of corrections, omitted words, proverbs, and place names. Kilian's love of the language is unmistakable, and on page after page of the dictionary he added words and comments in pencil. As he immersed himself in the book, his mind brought back images of walking through the Döhlen Hills, living with his relatives at Hochkirch, and basking in the lovely tranquility of the Kotitz parsonage and the Kotitz garden.[34]

FURTHER DIVISIONS

Just three years after the conventicle controversy ended with the reunification in 1867, Kilian faced another controversy that was based on a different dimension, but fed on the first. The first division had assaulted one of Kilian's principles – basic Lutheranism; and now the second division confronted his second principle – the Wendish heritage based on the Wendish language.

The threat came, not from English, the language of his new home, but from German. It was one more engagement in the age-old conflict between Teuton and Slav once fought in mortal combat in central Europe and now reenacted in a final skirmish in the post oak forest of Texas. Even though Kilian emphasized Wendish in church and school, he had made some concessions to German because there were some Germans in the migrating group and he preached to them in German, already when they were crossing the Atlantic Ocean. In Texas neighboring Germans joined the congregation and there were those Wendish families in which one spouse was German or in which they believed that German was a more valuable language to learn than

Wendish. Concessions were also made in the services and voters' assembly.

The Wendish congregation, readily accommodated those who preferred German. From the beginning, Kilian preached in both languages on Sundays and holy days, just as he had done in Europe. Then in 1856 some youngsters were confirmed in German. That rite was held on Good Friday and the Wendish confirmation was on the traditional Palm Sunday. By 1870 the German confirmation class was larger than the Wendish class. In 1866 the Voters' Assembly experimented with one meeting in German and the other in Wendish. That procedure proved unworkable, so the next year they conducted the meetings in German, and Kilian translated the minutes into Wendish for those who did not know German, and comments made by Wends he translated into German.[35]

The roots of the controversy go back to the time of Lehnigk when he taught school. Before that, Kilian not only looked after the congregation, but also taught the school with fifty some children. Kilian was happy to relinquish his school obligations because doing so enabled him to direct his energies to the pastoral ministry, and the parents were pleased with a teacher whose entire attention could be directed toward their children. When Lehnigk moved away, the parents lobbied for a new teacher, but Kilian had misgivings about calling one "until the Lehnigk storm has passed over."[36] When the storm ended, the congregation asked the synod for a teacher.

Ernst Leubner, a fresh graduate from Addison, was inducted on August 30, 1868 as teacher and cantor. No one questioned his work in the classroom, even though he could not teach Wendish – only German and English. Kilian assisted by instructing the pupils in Wendish twice a week. Leubner's leadership in music, however, was not acceptable. Even though he was given the opportunity to learn the Wendish liturgy and the technique of adapting the organ accompaniment to the Wendish way of singing, he refused. He maintained that the responsibility was not his to learn Wendish, but rather the congregation's to learn German. Kilian maintained that missionaries must learn the language of their people.

Because of the impasse, Carl Teinert, the long-standing organist and cantor, retained his position for a time. But then Leubner insisted that the position was his by virtue of the call. The entire problem came to the Voters' Assembly and the debate was intense with one side supporting the Wendish way and the other side supporting Leubner and the German way. During the congregational debate, Kilian took a neutral position. But the German minority was organized, and because many Wends did not attend, the German minority successfully voted to turn over the position to Leubner. The old fault lines opened for another controversy.

Third Serbin church
Source: Texas Wendish Heritage Society

Just as the first controversy was resolved with the aid of a synodical representative, so once again both sides looked to the Synod. The visitor, in this instance was The Rev. Theodore Brohm from New Orleans. Kilian sent him instructions for the journey. After making his way to Galveston, Brohm should find the firm of J. Kaufmann & Co. if he needed assistance. If he needed help in Houston, he should locate Pastor Braun. From Houston he could travel on the railroad to Brenham and find lodging with the baker, Johann Neuman. Because the railroad stopped at Brenham, it was necessary for him to take the stage to Round Top, LaGrange, and Winchester. As Winchester was eight miles from Serbin the last leg could be made by wagon, which Kilian could send, or Brohm could hire. Brohm's compensation depended on his finding. If his decision was agreeable to both sides, they would divide the cost. However, if one side was pleased with the judgment and the other not, he would receive compensation from the group that was pleased. Nothing was said about compensation if neither side was pleased.

Following Kilian's instructions, Brohm arrived and listened to both sides on May 15 and 16. No common ground could be found and a division seemed to be the only alternative. On May 22, 1870, Kilian tendered his resignation effective in September. The Wendish majority then voted to call Kilian back as their pastor and he accepted. When September arrived they asked for Leubner's resignation, and that placed Kilian back in the classroom. The members of the German faction, in the meantime, organized themselves into a congregation, asked the Missouri Synod for a pastor, and formally separated on September 25, 1870, taking Leubner as their teacher.

But the two congregations were not clearly divided along ethnic lines. Kilian's Wendish congregation also included some Germans while the German congregation included the earlier conventicalists who were Wends and also those Wends who preferred German. So the controversy that began over language did not divide strictly according to language. An amiable division of the property was accomplished, however, with the assistance of lawyers – two from LaGrange and two from Bastrop. The departing group received the land of the earlier St. Peter's congregation, the old organ, and one thousand dollars. Kilian's congregation, now changing its name to St. Paul, received most of the property and the unfinished stone church. Kilian lost approximately one-third of the congregation, although in the five years following the division, he baptized an average of twenty-eight children a year as compared to thirty-one for the five years prior to the schism.[37] So Kilian's congregation held its own, even though it lost some potential growth. The division did not create good will or divide the labor. Because both ethnic groups were represented in both congregations, Kilian and the new pastor continued to preach two sermons each Sunday – one in German and one in Wendish. Problems of a different nature arose. What would happen, for example, if a person from one congregation married a person from the other? Which church would they attend? Only the cemetery was shared by both.

Just as in the first controversy, this controversy disrupted the important project of building a new house of worship. Within six years after the wooden church was finished, the congregation had decided to construct a larger building and to use the wooden church as their school. The new church was to be made of stone and was to have seating for six-hundred people. Construction, however, was delayed because of an epidemic of fever. Finally, on January 24, 1867, a contract was signed and on May 5th the cornerstone was laid. By October 23, 1868, the tower was completed. But then the controversy with Leubner arose and while that was going on, a portion of the congregation living at Fedor, more than twenty miles distant, decided to form yet another congregation. So in March, with the creation of the Fedor congregation and then in September with the formation of St. Peter, Kilian lost vital financial support and the construction lagged. The membership declined from 770 to 470.[38]

Even worse, in Kilian's estimation, was the fact that the Missouri Synod in both cases accepted both of the new congregations into fellowship without consulting Kilian. Admittedly the Fedor people lived a good distant away to justify a separate church, but Kilian thought they should stay. Kilian discounted the distance and urged Walther not to send a pastor to Fedor. Both new congregations called pastors, and each received a Lusatian-born clergyman who had attended a Missouri Synod seminary. The role of the Synod in aiding and abetting the two congregations was especially galling to Kilian and he wrote, "One German is one German and a Sorb is nothing. This new congregation [St. Peter's], that was set up for things German…has built a new church and parsonage, opposite me that stares me in the face."

The Rev. John Pallmer, a Wend from Baden, Missouri, who had been called even before the formal separation took place, accepted the call to Serbin and arrived in October 1870. Originating from

Bederwitz, he had migrated to the United States on his own and accepted the parish at Baden after graduation from the seminary in 1869. The District President asked Kilian to install the new pastor, a task Kilian found difficult, but one which he "obediently" carried out. Kilian accepted the new reality and reminded the congregation of Abraham and Lot, who went their separate ways but maintained their unity of faith. Later Kilian would comment that "to my own humiliation an outsider became a proprietor with equal rights in my backyard."[39] Pallmer served his congregation in both German and Wendish until his death three years later, in 1873.

While St. Peter's constructed a new frame church, St. Paul's, in all likelihood stimulated by the competition, resumed the construction and dedicated its new stone church on December 3, 1871. That church, still in use 130 years later, has become the symbol of Wendish community and of Kilian's achievement.

The personal relations between Pallmer and Kilian, neighboring pastors, started cooly but ended cordially. Even though Gerhard wrote to his father that Pallmer was highly regarded in St. Louis and that his wife, a former nurse, was a good person, initially there was little social contact between the two men. On occasion, Pallmer sent bitter messages to Kilian, but Kilian did not answer. Kilian also suggested to Synod that if Synod would call Pallmer away from Serbin, the two congregations would most likely unite. But the two men had too much in common for the aloofness to continue. Pallmer's notes became less strident, and soon the two men spent more time together.

Tragedy struck on the evening of July 4, 1873 when Pallmer's wife died at childbirth. Pallmer, grief-stricken, asked Kilian to conduct the funeral the next day, and Kilian consented. Then Pallmer became ill and he asked Kilian to take over the official acts of the congregation. As Pallmer lay ill, Kilian visited him. But then Kilian himself became ill, and Pallmer came to visit Kilian. So while relations were strained between the two congregations, the two pastors maintained a friendship and so did the young people of the two congregations.

After Pallmer's death, St. Peter called Pastor A. D. Greif, who preached only in German. Kilian, feeling his age and declining health, believed that the only sensible solution was to divide the congregations on linguistic lines so that both pastors would preach only one sermon each Sunday. Kilian's proposal did not materialize. St. Peter's Wends worshiped in German, and Kilian's St. Paul used both Wendish and German. Pastor Greif occupied St. Peter's for three years and then Pastor Geyer, an older man from Missouri, became the pastor.[40]

Even before the new St. Paul's church was dedicated in 1871, yet another outlying settlement at Warda decided that Serbin was too far away. People living in that area, about half a dozen miles from Serbin, attended both St. Peter and St. Paul. The first step was the establishment of a school so the trip on school days was reduced in length. But there were misunderstandings and at the urging of Teinert, who had been replaced as music leader, they formed their own congregation. Because they had not been given peaceful releases from the Serbin congregations, the Missouri Synod would not supply them with a pastor. Warda in turn applied to the Texas Synod and received a pastor. He died shortly thereafter and in 1878 Pastor Koestering came from St. Louis and resolved the problem and once again the Missouri Synod admitted a congregation composed largely of former St. Paul members and provided it with a pastor.

Given all the new parishes one would assume that each would remain small and insignificant. But after the Civil War, immigration resumed and many Sorbs wended their way to Serbin to add to the membership or they made their homes in the surrounding areas and affiliated with Serbin's daughter congregations. In 1870, for example, 175 more people took communion at St. Paul than had taken it the previous year.

Kilian accepted these new congregations with grumbling grace and learned to appreciate the collegiality of the pastors, a quality that had been absent for years. In 1872 St. Paul hosted the Missouri Synod pastors in Texas as they held their first conference. Kilian invited Pastor Braun, who was not a member of the Synod, but Braun did not attend. Kilian reported that "At first I had no desire for a pastoral conference because of the concerns of which I will relate later. But the conference was splendid!" Four of the seven pastors could preach in Wendish: Kilian, Pallmer, Proft and Andreas Schmidt from Black Jack Springs. Kilian was elected to the chairmanship on the condition that he could speak whenever it pleased him. The younger pastors were pressured to preach in the two Serbin congregations, so Schmidt preached in Wendish at St. Paul, enabling Kilian to attend the German sermon preached by Pastor Klindworth at St. Peter. Kilian reported that his former opponents greeted him with smiles.

During Kilian's lifetime the two congregations remained separate, and after Pallmer's death Kilian became the colleague of first Pastor Greif and then Pastor Geyer. During the pastorate of Kilian's son, the congregations did unite. Symbolically, as if to purge their memories of an unpleasant chapter of Serbin's history, the members burned the congregational minutes of St. Peter's.[41]

MILLENNIALISM

Kilian disagreed with the Missouri Synod on the theological issue of millennialism or chiliasm and stated, "I am not at home in my own synod." Millennialism has many scenarios and variations, but in general it maintains that prior to Christ's return on Judgment Day, the world will end and there will be a thousand years of rule by Christ. The major source of support for millennialism is in the last book of the Bible, Revelation, written by St. John living in exile on Patmos Island. Millennialism was a common topic for discussions in nineteenth century Lutheran circles and even served as the issue that divided the Australian Lutherans for many decades. Twentieth century Lutherans, however, with the exception of a few months at the end of the second millennial, devoted little attention to millennialism outside of Bible class studies of Revelation.

The Missouri Synod, ever since its founding, adhered to the position on millennialism as stated in Article XVII of the Augsburg Confession. There, millennialism was condemned and the condemnation was based on a statement of Jesus that He did not come to establish a kingdom on earth. Kilian, though a staunch adherent of the Lutheran Confessions, believed that the teaching should not be dogmatically prohibited but that it should be considered an open topic, open for discussion, until the Synod could make a "firm symbolic resolution" against it. In 1857 Kilian informed Walther that he was neutral on the topic. But that same year after Pastor G. A. Schieferdecker, President of the Western District of the Missouri Synod, was ousted because of his stand on millennialism, Kilian objected and planned to prepare a written statement.[42]

Kilian differentiated between a kingdom and a reign. He believed that the concept of a specific thousand year kingdom was based on a Jewish idea and was justifiably rejected in the Augsburg Confession. But he did believe that there would be a reign of a thousand years when Christ and "identified holy ones" would rule and institute a powerful reformation. During that time all the heathen would be converted and then Judgment Day would follow. Millennialism was neither a burning issue nor a divisive one in Kilian's Serbin congregation, but it was a topic that Kilian pursued from the Schieferdecker expulsion to the end of his life.

Kilian was battling on two fronts in 1858: the conventicles in his neighborhood and millennialism with the Synod. But Walther and the Synod never joined the battle with him on millennialism and clearly agreed with him on the conventicles. Evidently Kilian did not pose as a threat with his millennialism, so why bother debating the topic, much less removing him from Synod? The difference between Schieferdecker and Kilian was that Schieferdecker was the president of the Western district, and Kilian was a parish pastor in Texas – on the geographical fringes of the synod. So Kilian could write and talk on millennialism all he liked if he had strength left over from the conventicle controversy.

He completed his treatise on "The Perception of Chiliasm" by October 1858 and mailed a copy to Walther. There was no action against him, and no record of any response. In 1859 he took time to describe all his controversies to an old friend, Pastor Clamor Schuermann in Australia.[43] Schuermann, like Walther, agreed on the conventicles, but was actually on the opposite side of Kilian on the millennial question. Then in 1860, Kilian attended the convention in St. Louis and declared his opposition to Missouri's closing consideration of the issue. Again, no reaction. When the Civil War began in 1861 Kilian's geographical isolation was greater than ever and so were his opportunities for intellectual exchange. He could still send letters to Europe, forwarding them through Mexico, but not all were answered. In a letter to Walther in 1865, after the end of the war, he again included a comment on millennialism, but received no direct response.

Walther, however, wrote to Kilian questioning some of Kilian's comments that appeared in a Saxon journal *Kirche- und Schulblatt*. In a previous letter to Europe, Kilian had expressed his dissatisfaction with the Missouri Synod for its stand on millennialism and implied that he had "distanced" himself from the Synod. An excerpt from the letter appeared in the Saxon journal and came to Walther's attention, so after the end of the Civil War Walther wrote to Kilian and requested an explanation. To make amends, Kilian clarified his views in a letter to the Saxon journal in which he not only heaped high praise on the Missouri Synod, but also reported that he could never consider being a member of any other synod and had even encouraged his congregation in Serbin to join the Synod. Kilian's retraction seems to have satisfied Walther; but later, in 1874, Kilian reported that his once friendly correspondence with Walther had ceased and that since 1867 Walther had not responded to any of Kilian's letters. "Not a single syllable."[44]

In January 1873, however, after a seven year hiatus, Kilian received a letter from Pastor Rudolph Richter, who was an old university roommate and who then occupied the pulpit in Kilian's old parish of Kotitz. Richter included a published commentary he had written on Revelation. Kilian acknowledged the gift but responded that he was "not always in the frame of mind for such reading material and also does not always have the time." A month later, however, Kilian forwarded the book to Walther and asked if he could help find a distributor for the book in America.

Richter's material helped rekindle Kilian's interest in millennialism, and in 1874, at the pastoral conference, Kilian delivered an essay on that topic. The essay was intended to stimulate discussion, and it did, but the opposition was strong, and the debate heated. The pastoral conference had been founded only two years earlier and the younger pastors had treated Kilian with deference then, and there had been a pleasant spirit of collegiality. The current conference ended on a discordant note and the issue lay dormant, but smoldering, for the next two years. During that time, in 1875 Schieferdecker, whom Kilian had so staunchly defended, retracted his position on millennialism, but Kilian carried on. In 1876 Kilian "felt compelled, before my death, to put forth a testimony 'Hope for Better Times for the Church on Earth....'" At the next conference, which met at Cypress, near Houston, on September 17, 1876, Kilian preached on that theme, and again there was intense opposition in the open discussion, and again there was no resolution.

At the 1877 spring conference, however, the pastors decided that there had been enough open discussion and that Kilian must agree or disagree on the matter. They prepared certain statements and asked Kilian to respond only with a specific "Yes" or "No." Kilian resented the attempt to corner him, called the meeting an Inquisition, and refused to participate in any more discussions. Under pressure from his fellows, Kilian eventually drew up twenty theses that he was willing to defend. These theses and a report were sent to the President of the Western District. Before further actions followed, Kilian, in mid-January 1878, met with a representative or Visitor from the District and followed the example of Schieferdecker by retracting his earlier positions.

He never raised the issue again in Missouri Synod circles, but he continued to hold his view and wrote about the topic to a member of the Iowa Synod, Dr. G. Fritschel. One week after he had recanted, Kilian wrote a letter to Fritschel summarizing his life and his conflict over millennialism, but he said nothing about renouncing his views. Instead he said, "All that [sermon and twenty theses] so stirred up the spirits in the Synod, that they ordained a visitation to be held in January 1878 in order to quench the increasing fire of biblical hope."[45] Kilian could not exclude millennialism from his mind, and most likely held his views until his dying day.

Kilian's fixation with millennialism is difficult to explain. It was not a burning issue of faith, and the Augsburg Confession, one of those confessions he so staunchly affirmed, disparaged the concept. Neither was it a topic that aroused or excited the congregation. His repeated references and defenses of it, when no one seemed to care, consumed time that could more profitably have been spent in creative ways similar to those he had demonstrated in Kotitz.[46] And his persistence jeopardized his standing with his Synod and his relationship with his fellow pastors. There was almost a perversity about his fixation, so that even when he was finally cornered and when he agreed to his error, he continued a correspond secretly with a sympathetic theologian.

Quite possibly his attention to millennialism tells us more about the inner Kilian. One aspect of that concept is its appeal to people whose life is not fulfilling and whose goals are unmet, those who feel injustice and oppression and look for a time here on earth which will right the wrongs. We can only imagine how Kilian felt. He had given up his lovely little parish in Kotitz, where he translated, composed, and published, and received in exchange a two-room log cabin in Texas where he taught school every day, lived on meager funds, and quarreled with malcontents. When he proposed returning to Europe, he learned that he was not wanted. He was a prisoner in a prison of his own making; and, short of heaven, only the millennium would make life on earth satisfying. His strong defense of a prophecy that envisioned eventual victory and "biblical hope" can only show that in the closing years of his life, he must have realized that hopes of resurrecting sound Lutheranism in Europe were unfulfilled and so were his efforts to build a stronghold in Texas. There was "no hope for better times for the church on earth," except in the millennium.

KILIAN'S CHANGING SENSE OF SATISFACTION

Motivation for any action, including that of migration, is generally founded not on a single impulse, but on several. Kilian's decision to leave Germany was based partly on his desire to escape from one situation as well as his dream to accomplish another goal in America. Kilian's sense of purpose and satisfaction fluctuated from the moment he arrived until his death.

His first position was one of optimism. He knew there would be problems, but he had a sense of achievement. Already in March 1855, just three months after he arrived, he said: "I notice that I will have opposition here just as I had in the old fatherland. Yet I hope to find comfort here." Those early years were years of uncertainty. The congregation was scattered from Houston to Serbin, the first crops were not planted in time, everyone was scrambling for shelter, and then there were two years of inadequate rain. Finally, by the end of 1858, he felt secure and could say, "I have just now gained the impression that the Lutheran Church will take root in Texas."

He also defended the American separation of church and state and rejected the Old World's state church. In America hypocrisy was unnecessary; no one needed to pretend that he was a believer. The worst mockers and atheists were not native Americans, but Europeans born to a system of a compulsory religious environment. "In no way would I like to trade the sorry legalism, which has spread within the state churches of Germany for our separation of church and state." He liked the political system, he liked the religious possibilities, and he found personal contentment. "After being here a few years, one settles down and I like it very much." And he prided himself in his nineteen head of cattle, sixteen hogs, and one horse.[47]

But then came the depressing conflict with the conventicelists, and the separation of church and state lost some of its luster because it placed the lay people in power which he called "the lay papacy." Kilian began to think that a different person would be more suited for his post. He wrote letters to Germany, inquiring about such a person, and his friends in Germany sensed a desire to return to his homeland. Kilian, in 1859, asked Lehmann to write a letter denying these rumors. "For in the land of the Sorbs it is being told that our pastor wants to leave us and has mailed letters there asking that a place be found for him there. He [Kilian] has ordered me to oppose those rumors and those of his friends to whom he once sent confidential letters in which he asked for an aide or anything similar, all of which could have given cause to these vexing reports...." There is a hint of remorse in his thoughts for leaving Europe.

If Kilian did indeed have thoughts of finding a replacement so that he could return to Europe, those thoughts were frustrated by the American Civil War. But even before the war ended, his thoughts of remorse about leaving Europe had metamorphosed into a yearning to return to Europe. And he made his desire to return to Europe public in a letter to the church council in Saxony: "...because I have to teach 50 children, my official duties are so demanding that in the future I need to look for a tranquil place in my old fatherland." "In addition to this among my 5 children; I have 3 sons – one twelve, one six and one four, for whom I would like to provide a higher education for which no real possibility exists over here except that I could instruct them myself in religion. Also I am troubled by the loneliness and solitude in this place in that I am not able to associate with anyone commensurate with my educational background. That is why my first concern is to hear whether or not you could and would offer me a Wendish parish if I would return to my native homeland."[48]

Yet he would never desert the colony without arranging for spiritual and educational direction, so during the Civil War, when Texas was cut off from its synodical ties, he tried to establish a liaison with the Saxon state church, hoping that it would provide Serbin with teachers – and with teachers who could also preach. But nothing resulted from the overture, and when the war ended and communication between North and South was resumed, Kilian encouraged the congregation to join him in an affiliation with the Missouri Synod and with it a source of pastors and teachers.

In the spring of 1867 as the conventicle controversy was shifting to the synodical level, Kilian lost his spirit. He was tired of controversy, and said: "Here in the wilds of Texas I am attacked on the one side by a heathenish lack of restraint and on the other side by a Jewish legality, that I can hardly bear it any longer. In such a predicament I will become either devastated or missing and presumed dead. I have advanced in knowledge, but with my life I have not kept up with my knowledge nor reached my ideals." He was not really at home in Saxony or Prussia, but neither was he at home in the Missouri Synod. "I wish I could be alone again and do some writing. But even more I yearn to find rest somewhere."

If there were no vacant parishes in Europe, perhaps there was a position in the northern states. In such a "morose mood" he asked Director Lindemann for "a quiet position in the North." He then wrote to Walther about the possibility of obtaining an appointment as lecturer at the St. Louis Seminary or a pastorate of a Czech congregation. Unsuccessful with those feelers, he notified two clergymen in the Iowa Synod of his availability. He had misgivings about the Iowa Synod's stand on the office of the ministry and warned them that he himself could not become a member of the synod unless the synod changed its position on that teaching. While he was in the process of reducing his chances of receiving a call because of his misgivings, he added two additional requirements: no travel to daughter congregations and a room for study.[49]

His persistent and repeated requests went unfulfilled in both Europe and the United States and he realized that he would find no relief. "My own punishment remains that I must continue as the pastor in Serbin." He admitted to himself that "I do not feel a real incentive to return to the land of the Sorbs. And as I again thought of returning to the land of the Sorbs, no one wanted me and no one would take my place. That had to be that way. Sadowa [a battle where Napoleon was defeated] has now dashed and choked my earlier desires."[50] His desire for escape gave way to dejection, and Serbin became his Elba.

Yet Kilian, like Napoleon, still harbored some hope for escape. In 1872 Gerhard's installation as teacher stabilized that office, and soon there were three Wendish clergymen in Texas who could assume the Serbin pulpit. Even with Gerhard teaching school and relieving Kilian from that burden, he could not forget his homeland. "Here I feel constantly a stranger." In 1874 Kilian wrote, "I would very much like to see my Kotitz residence, the fruit trees in the parsonage garden – the birch – the pine." But before Kilian could implement any change, the depression following the Panic of 1873 weakened the economy, and the land he held lost its value and a loan he made, could not be collected. He could not risk leaving the little security that he had. His health also improved and his spirits lifted.

At the same time Europe once more became less attractive. "I hear that the former oath of the clergy has been done away with and that a new vow formula was introduced which weakens the right or power of the Lutheran Confessions. You can be sure that my conscience would never agree to such chaos…But I do not have a call to the land of the Sorbs. And to undertake such as that without a call is dangerous."

Realizing that he had no choice but to remain in Texas, Kilian contemplated at least a visit to Lausitz before the frailty of age would prohibit it. But again financial constraints, especially because of the loss associated with Warda, prevented even one little journey to the land of his birth. "I must continue on with my lonely lifestyle and say

Third Serbin Church
Contemporary View
Source: George Nielsen

with Solomon, 'All is vanity and full of lamentation.'"[51] Serbin became his St. Helena.

Kilian, however, unlike Napoleon, did not brood, but embraced America as his home. In 1879, in one of his last letters to Europe, Kilian praised Texas as a land of opportunity for poor people who were law-abiding and willing to work, and for religious freedom where the government did not interfere in matters of the church. "I am glad that I am in America."[52]

KILIAN: AN APPRAISAL

When Kilian signed his letters he wrote: "Johann Kilian, P." The letter behind his name stood for pastor, or in German, *Pastor* (pah STORE) – shepherd. There are other German names for clergyman including *Geistlicher* (GUYST-lich-her) – spiritual one, *Pfarrer* (FAR rurh) – person of the parish, and *Seelsorger* (ZALE-zor-girr) – one who cares about the soul. Whether *Pastor* was a conscious choice or merely part of Kilian's tradition is not known. Under either circumstance, he viewed himself as a shepherd.

If he saw himself as a shepherd, he not only looked after each individual sheep, but he also fought predators who had designs on his flock. So he spent some of his time fighting battles to provide a secure environment for the flock and some of the time caring for the sheep. How successful was he in either role, and how did he view his own career?

As a militant shepherd, Kilian looks very much like a reformer – someone who wants to change things for the benefit of all. Dear to his heart were the Scriptures and the Lutheran Confessions, documents he read, studied, and translated. When conditions in Europe threatened the flock and its relations to the Scriptures and the Lutheran Confessions – the basis of their faith, he became the reformer. Whether working with a nobleman to bring social and economic reform, jousting with German church leaders to bring religious material to the Wendish people, or opposing the Prussian rulers by serving a separatist church, Kilian was trying to improve the religious environment. In Europe his role as reformer, in spite of limited successes, energized him and gave him a sense of mission.

But the role of reformer also led him into difficulties. It led him to America in the hope that the flock could flourish when not stalked by a predatory government. Instead, Kilian experienced ironies that another reformer, Martin Luther, experienced. Once he fought the establishment and survived, he became the establishment and had to defend the status quo. Luther's Anabaptists and Zwinglians were Kilian's conventicalists and Germanizers. When he joined the Missouri Synod for collegiality, he found colleagues that did not agree with him on the millennium and the formation of daughter congregations. And then when the environment seemed secure for the sheep, some sheep did not heed the master's voice.

Kilian's discovery, made near the end of his life, was one other reformers and single-minded people have made. Perfection is elusive. The state church had advantages and disadvantages, but so did the independent churches. Congregational members can be supportive or subversive. The Synod was both helpful and restrictive. He wrote, "We have no abiding city...I was not at home in Europe and neither am I at home here." Toward the end of his life, when he was asked about splitting off from the Missouri Synod, Kilian said, "Consequently every separation brings us out of one frying pan into another. I therefore do not know any other position than the counsel of God."[53]

Kilian's correspondence is heavily weighted with many pages related to the militant shepherd or reformer role and not about his care of individuals. That caring function of his ministry was simply taken for granted. But one cannot help being impressed with his meticulous records, beginning with his first parish, on through the passenger list of the *Ben Nevis*, and concluding with the Serbin congregation. He knew his flock. He taught the children in elementary school, instructed the adolescents in confirmation classes, baptized children, married couples, and buried the dead. He listened to confessions, visited the homes of the parishioners, spoke with them after church, preached two sermons in two different languages on Sundays and also the two festival days after the major events of the church year. All this while, he worked in the field and garden, tended his horse and cows, lived in a log cabin with no study, where his bedroom was also the living room, and he remained a loving husband and father.

If Kilian had been asked to evaluate his life, he most likely would have considered it a failure. His letters do not reflect any satisfaction in his work, nor did he reveal any pride in his accomplishments. The shortcomings, real or imagined, eclipsed any joy he may have felt. He failed to preserve the large single Wendish congregation under his leadership and much of his life in Texas was marked by recrimination instead of amiable relationships. The struggle drained his energy and embittered his life. He fought a losing battle to maintain the Wendish ways, and instead of holding all the people within his congregation, he lost family after family to other communities and congregations.

The preoccupation with his failures to secure a safe environment clouded his perception when instead he should have rejoiced in his work day-by-day. In spite of what he may have considered failures, he and his congregation sowed a seed of Lutheranism in Texas. It was not Wendish, but it was Lutheran; and eventually the parishoners spoke neither Wendish or German but the language of their new homeland. His life had come full circle. His youthful dream of becoming a missionary to a foreign land, a dream he had abandoned, had became a reality, and the intermittent bickering and conflict prevented him from realizing it.

Kilian's tombstone in center; Mrs. Kilian's tombstone on the left
Source: Jack Wiederhoft

APPENDIX
SELECTED WRITINGS

[1851] Kilian to Doctor Adolph Harless, [Chief Clergyman of the Court] in Dresden [Weigersdorf]

Kilian, by leaving Kotitz to become the pastor in the independent congregation, gave up his ties to the Saxon state church. He did join the fellowship of the Old Lutherans, but he never developed intimate ties with any pastors of that group. Harless was a prominent theologian in the Saxon church and in this letter Kilian unburdens himself to a confidant and provides us with insights into his motivations.

Rev. Pastor and President!
Most respected Doctor!
Your friendly word spoken at Weicha, that "I should write you when I have something on my heart" encouraged me to share with you a double confidential disclosure. The one deals with my present situation, the second on the migration contemplated by many.

My *present situation*, Rev. Sir, can partly be seen from my articles *not* accepted by the "Saxon Church and School Journal," which the editor Hölemann from Leipzig, according to my wish, hopefully will send you soon or already has sent. I came here to Prussia partially because of pressure not to desert the people after the Saxon candidate Schmidt, a Wend, who had a call there declined it, to his and my detriment, and because no other Wend could be found who could and would serve them. The Prussian administration raised many obstacles to keep me away from the country, because they viewed me as a source of trouble in the area. I was finally admitted by the honorable minister Eichhorn on my promise not to proselytize, and to obtain the permission from Kotitz to serve the brethren here in this office. So from the spring of 1847, with the approval of the Kotitz patron and the church authorities at Bautzen, I looked after the congregation here in addition to the Kotitz parish, but because the impossibility to serve satisfactorily the unusual and exhausting double position, it became necessary to give up the parish at Kotitz and to give myself entirely to these congregations because I could be replaced in comfortable Kotitz but under the thorns here [in Prussia] there was no prospect of a successor. In the fall of 1848 I moved here, whereupon I was recognized by the state, after I, on my petition of 14 May 1848 for Prussian citizenship, was admitted as a lowly subject. The congregations of Weigersdorf and Klitten together with the branch congregations of Muskau, Spremberg and Cottbus, had been united into one parish as a result of my accession. So that is how the series of humble events that I encountered, reached a successful conclusion.

Now, however, I am hard-pressed with doubts. Because I can find no definite answer to the question if the departure from the Prussian state church was necessary before God or not. The separation of the first Christians from paganism and Judaism gives no clue, because our erring churches are still part of the universal *Christian church*, when it was also besieged by anti-Christian forces. After all we find that the church at the time of Elias, which worshiped Baal, only Elias had formally left the church, otherwise he would have known that in Israel 7,000 had not bent the knee to Baal. The 7,000 did not leave prior to Elias....

Why then did we begin the struggle? Not only for the path to salvation, for there is in the Union personal confessional freedom for the individual, for it has remained free, but for the confessional freedom of the *church*, for the rights of the confessing community. That leads to the question: Have we seized Elias' and Luther's call prematurely and from self-will, without considering the results? There is so much affectation and narrow-mindedness with us....

Many of us also make something of their being Lutheran and too many raise their own righteousness and become loveless toward other Lutherans who have different views, and hate and are hated. To that comes the frequently thoughtless and arrogant impulse to build magnificent churches, in which the initial excitement is mistakenly interpreted as strong faith, (but) often only produces irresponsibility. The latter has brought us a loathsome indebtedness under which the congregation must founder if no help arrives. For the inner affairs of the church become outwardly through it, and one has so much to do with thoughts of construction and need for money that the enthusiasm for the one thing that is needful, is cooled and under the aspiration for comfort and, at the least, is rent by hardship, disorder, and discord. The consequences of each justified church separation show themselves questionable, if one remains in the country....

As for the *question on emigration*, a vow made during my youth desiring to go into missions, has given me the constant inclination toward foreign heathen lands. For that reason I already went to Basel in the winter of 1837. My decision in favor of Lutheran truths and the unionistic nature of the Basel mission school prevented me from carrying out my plan, and the Lutheran mission school at Dresden under Wermelskirch was just coming into existence. That is why I took the pastoral position at Kotitz offered to me. But I confess that I was never truly at home in this land. The present emigration now arouses my yearning anew, and I hope through joining an emigrant association to become useful for a mission, especially because I have misgivings here and am troubled over our church conditions and spiritual deterioration. I miss terribly in Prussia as well as in Saxony, the full *religious freedom* which Dr. Rudelbach so powerfully proclaims. In 1842 I wanted to publish a Wendish journal for spiritual growth, but the Saxon Ministry of Culture gave me a negative reply without telling me if it was my person, or my Lutheran position, or my Wendishness. So my general efficacy has been curtailed, and now the false non-religious Wendishness is placed in the path to the detriment of my people, that I cannot confront partly because of poverty, partly because of oppression, partly from lack of time....

Now God has opened the doors for mission and for religious freedom: can one be blamed if he goes, before he is too late? Indeed I dare not try to persuade anyone in an optional act, if he goes or if he stays. For it can go badly for the emigrant and, certainly, just as badly for the one who stays here. But I can neither blame one who emigrates nor one who stays. However, I know that in the next year many Wends will migrate, those that are in half-despairing circumstances and by the dreary prospects of the present time which brought out their hopelessness. If their departure should not come to pass, then God will prevent it by sending a storm. In that act one will see God's finger, just as one can recognize God's finger in the present freedom to emigrate….

In this I have expressed my thoughts to your reverence concerning the two questions that bother me to your reverence, and await your instruction and comfort concerning them, I remain in the Lord.

Sincerely, your obedient Johann Kilian P.

Dauban, near Niesky

[trans. Mahling, Biar, G. Nielsen]

[1854] *Ben Nevis Passenger* List [University of Texas Archives]

We do not know the conditions under which this copy of the passenger list was compiled. Passenger lists, generally, were not made in such detail and were deposited at the port receiving the passengers. Unfortunately, most records of ships arriving at Galveston in the 19th century were destroyed in a hurricane so no comparison can be made with the official list. Dr. Joseph Wilson, who has made an extensive study of Kilian's list, concludes that this list was probably initiated by an employee of the shipping contractor and completed and amended by Kilian. The initial list was made prior to August 1854, retained by Kilian, and then used by him for his records until 1868. Information in brackets has been included by the author.

No.	Family Head	Family Members	Status	City or Village	Region	Birthday	Remarks
1.	Kilian	Johann	Pastor	Weigersdorf	Rothenburg	March 22, 1811	
		Maria [Gröschel]	Wife	"	"	July 1, 1823	
		Gerhardt August	Son	"	"	April 6, 1852	
		Hanna Gröschel	Sister-in-law	"	"	Sept. 24 1836	
2.	Neumann	J. Carl Edward	Cottager	"	"	April 5, 1816	
		Maria [Urban]	Wife	"	"	March 24, 1818	
		John Carl Aug.	Son	"	"	May 2, 1841	
		Aug. Fuerchteg.	Son	"	"	Aug. 14, 1846	
		Joh. Maria	Daughter	"	"	Dec. 21, 1848	
		Mar. Magdelene	"	"	"	Oct. 25, 1851	Died Sept. 19 at Liverpool
		Hanna	"	"	"	June 13, 1854	
3.	Arldt	Johann	Cottager	"	"	March 17, 1810	
		Agnes [Stary]	Wife	"	"	Aug. 24, 1811	
		Johann	Son	"	"	Nov. 6, 1842	
		Hanna	Daughter	"	"	Jan 2, 1846	
4.	Kiesling	Johann	[retired farmer]	"	"	Mar. 14, 1787	Died Oct. 17, 1854
		Hanna [Hanske]	Wife	"	"	1797	Died Oct. 18, 1854
		Johann	Son	"	"	Oct. 29, 1832	
		Magdalena	Daughter	"	"	Dec. 1835	
		Ernst	Son	"	"	April 16, 1839	
5.	Lehmann	Johann Traugott	Mill foreman	Dauban	"	[Oct. 29, 1818]	[original frayed] Single
6.	Lehmann	Carl	Mill owner	Dauban	Rothenburg	March 4, 1814	
		Magdalene [Bosche]	Wife	"	"	July 16, 1820	

89

No.	Surname	Given Name	Relation		Date	Notes
7.	Kieschnik	Andreas	Cottager	"	Nov. 13, 1828	
8.	Kieschnik	Johann	Cottager	"	April 1795	
		Agnes [Kalich]	Wife	"	April 28, 1795	
		Magdalene	Daughter	"	Dec. 2, 1830	
		Maria	Son	"	Jan. 7, 1834	
		Johann		"	Jan. 8, 1834	
		Agnes	Daughter	"	[Jan. 25, 1836]	[original frayed]
9.	Teinert	Johann Carl	Gardener	"	[Sept. 13, 1816]	[original frayed]
		Maria [Schneider]	Wife	"	–d. Nov. 27, 1854	at sea [age 38]
		August	Son	"	[Dec. 19, 1837]	
		Johann	"	"	May, 14, 1841	
		Ernest	"	"	[June 6, 1843]	
		Anna	Daughter	"	[Mar. 5, 1846]	
		Maria	"	"	Feb. 2, 1850	
		Magdalene	"	"	Sept. 22, 1852	
10.	Moerbe	Johann	Cottager	"	June 4, 1830	Did not migrate
		Hanna	Sister	"	---	
		Maria	Mother	"	---	
11.	Vogel	Christoph	Hand Worker	"	[1831]	
		[Agnes] [Jenke]	Wife	"	[1828]	
12.	Lowke	Andreas	Gardener	Reichwalde	Oct. 1, 1814	
		Anna [Schubert]	Wife	"	July 21, 1819 [1809]	
		Christoph	Son	"	July 27, 1839	
		Johann	"	"	Aug. 15, 1849	
		Maria	Daughter	"	Feb. 13, 1842	
		Johanna	"	"	Aug. 9, 1845	Died Oct. 10, 1854 [Q'town]

No.	Surname	Name	Relation	Place		Date	Notes
13.	Schmidt	Matthaus	Cottager		"	June 3, 1802	
		Rosina [Schneider]	Wife		"	April 16, 1801	
		Johann	Son		"	March 14, 1831	
		Maria	Daughter		"	July 28, 1836	
		Hanna	"		"	Oct. 30, 1839	
14.	Lorentsk	George	Cottager		"	Oct. 3, 1816	
		Elizabeth [Casper]	Wife		"	[Mar. 19,] 1815	
		Johann	Son		"	1838	
		Matthaus	"		"	Dec. 21, 1839	
		Andreas	"		"	Oct. 7, 1844	
		Magdalene	Daughter		"	Feb. 15, 1848	
		Hanna	"		"	Oct. 20, 1853	Died Jan. 21 1861
15.	Knippa	Johann	Cottager	Buchwalde	Hoyerswerda "	Sept 13, 1811	
		Christina [Schneider]	Wife	"	"	Oct. 16 [17] 1831	[torn page]
		Georg	Son	--	"	Oct. 1, 183	
		[Anna]	--	--	"	Dec. 30, 1843	
		[Johann]	--	--	"	Feb. 1, 1847	
		[Maria]	--	"	"	Dec. 2, 1853	
16.	Wukasch	[Matthes]	--	"	"	Aug. 31, 1789	
		[Matthes]	--	"	"	May 21 [29], 1823	
		[Anna] [Mrosack]	[Wife]	"	"	Jan. 6, 1818	
		[Johann]	[Son]	"	"	Sept. 3, 1846	
		[Georg]	[Son]	"	"	Sept. 7, 1847	
		Matthes	Son	"	"	Sept. 18, 1850	
		Marie	Daughter	"	"	Aug. 11, 1853	

No.	Name	Relationship	Place		Date	Notes
17. Lowke	Georg	Cottager	Kl. Radisch	"	April 2, 1811	
		Wife	"	"	April 9, 1810	
18. Hattas	Andreas	Cottager	Reichwalde	"	May 23, 1805	
	Maria [Tilscher]	Wife	"	"	[June] 1822	
	Christoph	Son	"	"	Feb. 27, 1849	
	Andreas	"	"	"	June 25, 1851	
	Hanna	Daughter	"	"	Oct. 24, 1853	
19. Schatte	Christoph	Cottager	"	"	April 24, 1825	
	Rosina	Wife	"	"	Aug. 17, 1832	
	Johann	Son	"	"	Nov. 14, 1849	Died Nov. 3, 1854
20. Kruper-Hohle	Johann	Gardener	Jahmen	Rothenburg	Jan 25, 1825	
	Rosina [Jurak]	Wife	"		1830	
	Johann	Son	"	"	Nov. 10, 1853	
	Hanna Hohle	Mother	"	"	Jan. 28, 1797	
	Magdalena Jurak	Wife's sister	Reichwalde	"	Oct. 1836	Died Oct. 5, 1854
21. Schatte called Mrosko	Matthaus	Cottager	Jahmen	"	June 14, 1802	Died Sept. 22, 1854 Liverpool
	Rosina [Wobaj]	Wife	"	"	Oct. 21, 1801	Died Sept. 18, 1854 Liverpool
	Hanna	Daughter	"	"	Nov. 18, 1827	Died Sept. 6, 1854 at 3 o'clock at Liverpool
	Johann	Son	"		April 27, 1837	
22. Becker	Georg	Baker	Jahmen	"	Dec 24, 1823	Died June 12, 1855 Buried June 14
	Rosina [Drosche]	Wife	"	"	July 25, 1826	
	Johann	Son	"	"	July 17, 1853	
	Matthes Drosche	Father-in-law	"	"	Aug. 16, 1786	

No. & Surname	Given name	Relationship	Origin		Birth date	Notes
23. Paulik	Jacob	Cottager	Klitten	"	Aug. 1, 1800	
	Agnes	Wife	"	"	Aug. 28, 1786	Died Mar. 1855
24. Iselt	Georg	Cottager	"	"	Sept. 18, 1814	
	Rosina [Bamsch]	Wife	"	"	Aug. 16, 1810	
	Hanna	Daughter	"	"	Feb. 12, 1847	
	Johann	Son	"	"	Dec. 25, 1852 [1853]	
25. Schatte	Johann	Cottager	"	"	April 4, 1825	Died on Ship, Sept. 30, 1854
	Rosina [Kiesetz]	Wife	"	"	Sept. 18, 1822	Died at Liverpl, Sept. 26, 1854
	Matthaus	Son	"	"	June 21, 1846	Died at Liverpl, Sept. 22, 1854
	Johann	"	"	"	June 27, 1848	Died on ship, Sept. 27, 1854
	Hanna	Daughter	"	"	Sept. 3, 1853	Died at Liverpl, Sept. 25 1854
26. Bartsch	Maria	Cottager widow	"	"	Dec. 14, 1782	
	Hanna	Daughter	"	"	May 29, 1811	
	Maria	"	"	"	Aug. 29, 1839	
	Rosina	"	"	"	Oct. 24, 1822	
27. Schubert	Johann	Cottager	"	"	Oct. 8, [Nov. 12] 1806	
	Magdalene [Petrik]	Wife	"	"	July 27, 1825	
	Hanna	Daughter	"	"	Sept. 21, 1835	
	Rosina	"	"	"	Oct. 4, 1838	
	Matthaus	Son	"	"	Dec. 24, 1841	
	August	"	"	"	Dec. 30, 1842	
	Agnes	Daughter	"	"	May 23, 1849	
	Johann	Son	"	"	May 9, 1852	
	Hanna	Widow	"	"	Nov. 20, 1776	Schubert's mother
28. Socke	George	Cottager	Kaschel	"	June 26, 1812	
	Hanna [Schiwart]	Wife	"	"	April 28, 1816	
	Maria	Daughter	"	"	Sept. 23, 1838	

	Surname	Name	Relationship			Date	Remarks
29.	Domaschka	Matthes	Gardener		"	Nov. 8, 1818	
		Hanna [Jurz]	Wife		"	March 22 [19], 1824	
		Rosine	Daughter		"	Oct. 31, 1843	
		Marie	"		"	Dec. 6, 1847	
		Hanna Jurz [Büttner]	Mother-in-law		"	1783	Died Aug 11, 1855 at 1 a.m. Buried same day
30.	Schubert	Johann	Gardener		"	July 25, 1825	
		Anna [Mitschke]	Wife		"	Oct 24, 1825	
		Hanna	Daughter		"	Jan. 29, 1853	
		Rosina Mattke	Step-daughter		"	Feb. 13, 1847	Died, 1855
		Maria Gubin	Mother		"	Dec. 24, 1793	
31.	Schubert	George	Gardener	Tauer	"	June [15], 1818	
		Rosina [Born]	Wife	"	"	Dec. 1816	
		Matthaus	Son	"	"	July 6, 1839	War casualty
		Andreas	"	"	"	July 4, 1844	
		Johann	"	"	"	Feb. 15 [13], 1847	
32.	Schwoibe	Rosina	Maid	"	"	1830	
33.	Schoellnick	Johann	Retired estate owner	Dürrbach	"	Oct. 13, 1793	
		Hanna [Brydde]	Wife	"	"	Nov. 1793	
		Johann	Son	"	"	Feb. 2, 1830	Died Sept. 28, 1854, on ship
		Maria	Daughter	"	"	Mar. 28, 1829	Not aboard ship
34.	Schoellnick	Matthes	Half-farmer	"	"	Dec. 10, 1815	
		Anna [Moze]	Wife	"	"	1813 [July 9, 1808]	
		Johann	Son	"	"	July 9, 1838	
		Mattheus	"	"	"	March 23, 1848	Died Sept. 23, 1854, Liverpl
		Maria	Daughter	"	"	May 18, 1852	Died Nov. 14, 1854, 10 a.m.

No.	Surname	Given Name	Role	Place		Date	Notes
35.	Bamsch	Georg	Cottager		"	Nov. 17, 1813	
		Rosina [Schatte]	Wife		"	Jan. 7 [9], 1825	
		Johanna	Son		"	Jan. 20, 1852	
36.	Hollas	Johann	Hired Hand	Kl[ein] Oelsa	"	Feb. 18, 1821	
37.	Michalk	Hanna	Maid	"	"	May 8, 1825	
38.	Socke	Magdalena	Maid	Kl[ein] Oelsa	"	March 26, 1830	
39.	Schulze	Johann	Gardener	Förstgen	"	Oct. 30, 1801	
		Maria [Brade]	Wife	"	"	June 9, 1799	
		Johann	Son	"	"	Dec. 12, 1822	
		Mattheus	"	"	"	Mar. 13, 1832	
		Magdalena	Daughter	"	"	Mar. 31, 1843	
40.	Schuster	Mattheus	Laborer	"	"	May 17, 1815	
		Joh. Eleonore	Wife	"	"	July 17, 1832	
41.	Hocker	Georg	Cottager	"	"	April 12, 1805	
		Magdalene [Schulze]	Wife	"	"	1806	
42.	Vogel	Andreas	Cottager	"	"	Feb. 11, 1813	
		Agnes [Hansk]	Wife	"	"	Dec. 23, 1809	
		Johann	Son	"	"	Feb. 19, 1841	
		Ernst Gottlieb	"	"	"	Aug. 11, 1843	
		Maria	Daughter	"	"	Dec. 26, 1845	
		August	Son	"	"	Nov. 6, 1848	
43.	Kambor	Christoph	Cottager	Wunscha	"	Jan. 1800	
		Maria [Marko]	Wife	"	"	1802	Died of fever, June 16, 1855

Family	Name	Relation	Place	Born	Notes
	Hanna	Daughter		July 28, 1837	Died at Hamburg Sept. 10, 1854
	Rosina	"		Feb. 10, 1840	Died July 6, 1855
44. Schulze	Mattheus	Gardener		Feb 17, 1807	Died Nov. 20, 1954 [Atlantic]
	Hanna [Juritz]	Wife		1813	
	Rosina	Daughter		Aug. 15, 1833	
	Maria	"		Aug. 10, 1836	
	Johann	Son		July 8, 1840	
	Matthes	"		Jan. 1, 1843	
	Christoph	"		Mar. 30, 1874	
45. Zwahr	Andreas	Gardener	Sandförstgen	Dec. 5, 1813	Died Sept. 29, 1855
	Maria [Dzjnkin]	Wife	"	Oct. 16 [12], 1816	
	Hanna	Daughter	"	Mar. 20, 1845	
	Johann	Son	"	Dec. 24, 1846	
	Magdalena	Daughter	"	Mar. 15, 1849	
	Maria	"	"	Jan. 12, 1851	
	Agnes	"	"	Jan. 22, 1852	
	Christina	"	"	April 1, 1854	
46. Noak	Christoph	Cottager	Sandförstgen	Sept. 7, 1813	Buried Nov. 30
	Joh. Christiane [Pursche]	Wife	"	June 1, 1825	
47. Greulich	Johann	Cottager	Gebelzig	Oct. 5, 1822	
	Joh. Christiane [Brauer]	Wife	"	May 24, 1828	
	Hanna	Daughter	"	Oct. 16, 1849	
	Maria	"	"	Sept. 8, 1851	
48. Greulich	Andreas	Cottager		Oct. 5, 1821	Not aboard ship
	Magdalena	Wife		Oct. 28, 1829	

No.	Surname	Given Names	Status	Origin		Birth date	Remarks
49.	Pehse	Andreas	Cottager	Schadendorf	"	July 13, 1819	
		Hanna [Kunze]	Wife		"	Aug. 3, 1814	
		Matthius	Son		"	July 18, 1845	
		Joh. Gottlieb Franke	Stepson		"	Jan. 22, 1839	
		Andreas	"		"	Nov. 17, 1841	Died in Liverpl, Sept. 22, 1854
50.	Dunzer	Joh. Carl	Cabinet Maker	Muskau	"	Jan. 3, 1824	
		Christiane	Wife		"	Jan. 6, 1826	
		Caroline Bertha	Daughter		"	Dec. 24, 1852	
51.	Winkler	Joh. Carl August	Baker		"	Aug. 16, 1823	Not aboard ship
52.	Kohl	Joh. Gottlieb	Potter		"	Oct. 20, 1802	
		Joh. Ernstina	Wife		"	May 12, 1827	
		Carl Gottlieb	Son		"	May 2, 1842	
		Joh. Paulus	"		"	June 4, 1852	Died Sept. 30, 1854
		Joh. Ernstina Bertha	Daughter		"	Jan. 31, 1854	
53.	Patschke	Carl August	Cottager	Kolpen	Hoyerswerda	Dec. 19, 1818	
		Hanna [Matthias]	Wife		"	April 22, 1826	
		Maria	Daughter		"	Feb. 11, 1854	
54.	Casper	Georg	Cottager		"	June 2, 1816	
		Magdalena [Schneider]	Wife		"	[Aug. 6] 1823	
		Maria	Daughter		"	Sept. 13, 1845	
		Johann	Son		"	April 1, 1849	
		Traugott	"		"	Aug. 2, 1851	
		Andreas	"		"	May 12, 1854	
55.	Prellop	Matthes	Cottager	Geislitz	"	Oct. 7, 1822	
		Dorothea [Schneider]	Wife		"	1827	
		Johann	Son		"	Dec. 2, 1851	

No.	Surname	Given	Relationship	Place	Province	Date	Notes
56.	Kolba	Christian	Half-farmer	Neudorf		May 22, 1830	
		Maria [Casparik]	Wife	"		[Oct. 21, 1826] 1827	
		Maria	Daughter	"		Oct. 22, 1851	Died 1855
		Traugott	Son	"		Oct. 25, 1853	Died May 28, 1855 of high fever
57.	Kasper	Christian	Cottager	"		Jan. 22, 1854	
		Dorothea [Linack]	Wife	"		1823	
		Matthes	Son	"		Dec. 4, 1850	
58.	Zoch	Christian	Half-farmer	Spreewitz		Dec. 13, 1825	
		Maria [Schneider]	Wife	"		Nov. 3, 1821	
		Hans	Son	"		Oct. 17, 1847	
		Johanna	Daughter	"		Feb. 27, 1851	
		Maria	"	"		Nov. 3, 1853	
59.	Casparik	Johann	Cottager	Zerre		Oct. 3, 1817	
		Hanna [Linack]	Wife	"		Feb. 1813	
		Anna	Daughter	"		April 29, 1844	
		Matthes	Son	"		Aug. 22, 1847	
		Christian Jatzlau	Stepson	"		Oct. 21, 1834	
		Hans	"	"		July 15, 1837	
		Maria	Stepdaughter	"		Feb. 20, 1841	
60.	Handrick	Georg	Cottager	Dubrauke	Saxony	Jan. 2, 1818	
		Johanna [Rek]	Wife	"	"	1820	
		Maria	Daughter	"	"	Oct. 10, 1851	
		Anna	"	"	"	Mar. 11, 1853	
61.	Fritzsche [Britsche]	Georg	Mason	"	"	Oct. 26, 1813 [1815]	Died and buried Dec. 6, 1854
		Johanna [Krischke]	Wife	"	"	1816	
		Maria	Daughter	"	"	Jan. 9, 1845	

	Given	Relation	Place		Birth	Death/Notes
	Andreas	Son		"	Sept. 11, 1846	Died Oct. 2, 1854
	Anna	Daughter		"	Dec. 20, 1848	Died Dec. 25, 1854 [Texas]
	Johann	Son		"	Sept. 25, 1851	Baptized on the ship
	Peter	"		"	Sept. 11, 1854	
62. Boehmer	George	Laborer	Dubrauke	"	1802	Not aboard ship
	Hanna	Wife	"	"	1797	(Money was reimbursed)
63. Kubitz	Johann	Gardener	"	"	Nov. 12, 1810	
	Maria [Reben]	Wife	"	"	May [1], 1822	
	Johann	Son	"	"	1842	
	Maria	Daughter	"	"	1845 [Feb. 24, 1849]	
64. Groeschel	August	Gardener	Särke near Weissenberg	"	July 22, 1847	Died Aug. 1, 1855 at 6:30 p.m.
	Andreas	Father	"	"	Oct. 3, 1793	
	Magdalena	Sister	"	"	Dec. 8, 1831	
	Agnes	"	"	"	April 9, 1839	
65. Miertschin	Andreas	Gardener	"	"	Nov. 22, 1809	Died on ship, Sept. 28, 1854
	Anna [Lehmann]	Wife	"	"	Oct. 1, 1809	Died Sept. 29, 1854, on ship
	Johanna	Daughter	"	"	Aug. 6, 1835	
	Maria	"	"	"	Feb. 23 [Dec. 25] 1840	
	August	Son	"	"	July 8, 1842	
	Andreas	"	"	"	Feb. 18, 1847	
	Carl	"	"	"	Feb. 3, 1849	
66. Reinhart "child"	Christiana	Joh. Miertschin's bride	Särke	"	April 19, 1834	Died Oct. 10, 1854
	August [Miertschin]	Son	---	"	Sept. 2, 1854	Died Oct. 6, 1854
67. Neitsch	Johann	Cottager	Särke	"	April 19, 1829	
	Maria [Symmank]	Wife	"	"	July 30, 1825 [1824]	
	August	Son	"	"	Oct. 30, 1852	Died Oct. 6, 1854

	Name	Occupation	Place	Country	Date	Notes
68. Basche	Maria	Embroidery worker	Brösa	"	June 3, 1833	Not Aboard ship
69. Moerbe	Ernst Adolph	Gardener	Klix	"	Aug. 6, 1824	
	Agnes [Symmy]	Wife	"	"	1826	
	Joh. Traugott	Son	"	"	Oct. 1, 1847	
	Andreas	"	"	"	June 22, 1849	Died Nov. 7, 1854
	Maria	Daughter	"	"	Nov. 2, 1852	Died Nov. 9, 1854
	Carolina Donath	Maid	---	Prussia	June 17, 1832	Not aboard ship
70. Simmank	Carl August	Cottager	Carlsbrun	Saxony	May 29, 1812	
	Ana Magdel.	Wife	"	"	Oct. 19, 1812	
	Herman Ernst	Son	"	"	1837	
	Ernstina Helen	Daughter	"	"	1839	
	Louise Amalie	"	"	"	Dec. 9, 1844	
	Ana Juliane	"	"	"	April 6, 1849	
71. Werthschütz	Carl Gottlieb	Weaver	"	"	Nov. 21, 1820	
72. Bensch	Andreas	Shoemaker	Kl. Dubrau	"	Sept. 5, 1829	
73. Symmank	Andreas	Cottager	Malschwitz	"	Sept. 28, 1821	
	Joh. Christiane [Fritsche]	Wife	"	"	[Sept. 15], 1827	
	Johann	Son	"	"	Aug. 31, 1848	Died Sept. 30, 1854, near Queenstown
	Andreas	"	"	"	Feb. 28, 1852	
	Peter	"	"	"	Oct. 27, 1854	
74. Urban	Johann	Gardener	Rackel	"	May 17, 1818	
	Anna [Kschidl]	Wife	"	"	June 1822	
	Maria	Daughter	"	"	Jan. 26, 1848	
	Hanna	"	"	"	Jan. 14, 1850	

No.	Surname	Given name	Occupation	Origin	Birth date	Notes
75.	Urban	Johann	Son	"	Jan. 6, 1852	
		Michael	Grinder	Weissenberg	June 18, 1830	
		Hana Christine	Wife	"	Dec. 1, 1829	
76.	Jannasch	Johann	Watchmaker	"	May 4, 1809	Died in Houston, Aug. 14, 1855
		Magdalene	Wife	"	Jan. 30, 1815	Died in Houston, Aug. 12, 1855
		Anna	Daughter	"	Mar. 6, 1835	Died in Houston, Aug. 18, 1855
		Johann	Son	"	May 10, 1839	
		Maria	Daughter	"	March 7, 1843	
		August	Son	"	Nov. 31, 1845	Died Dec. 10, 1854
		Ernst	"	"	July 5, 1850	Died Dec. 14, 1854
		Emil	"	"	July 8, 1852	[d. Dec. 11, 1854]
77.	Herbrig	Gotthelf Benjam.	Saw smith	"	Feb. 16, 1809	
		Joh. Christiane [Lehmann]	Wife	"	Oct. 15, 1823	
		Ernst Gotthelf	Son	"	Sept. 20 [21], 1847	
		Joh. Magdalene	Daughter	"	Jan. 10, 1852	
		Israel	Brother	"	Aug. 24, 1806	
78.	Besser	Joh. Carl Gottl.	Cottager	Weissenberg	Aug. 28, 1808	
		Hanna	Wife	"	------	
		Johanna	Daughter	"	Nov. 21, 1839	
79.	Jaeger	Carl Traugott	Mason	"	Sept. 23, 1832	
80.	Lehmann	Joh. Carl Aug.	Leathercraft, Harness maker	"	Aug. 10, 1837	
81.	Jannasch	Andreas	Watch maker	"	------	Died Dec. 12, 1854
82.	Urban	Andreas	Quarryman	Kubschuetz	Mar. 8, 1826	

No.	Surname	Name	Relation	Place	Date	Death
		Magdalena [Bowyer]	Wife	"	Mar. 2, 1822	
		Johann	Son	"	May 7, 1849	
		August	"	"	June 8, 1850	
		Ernst	"	"	June 12, 1852	Died Sept. 22, 1854 at Liverpool
		Peter	"	"	Jan. 28, 1854	
83.	Urban	Johann	Farmer	"	1787	Died Oct. 10, 1854
		Maria	Wife	"	1794	Died early Aug. 1855
		Jacob	Son	"	1837	
84.	Kurijo	Michael	Gardener	Wurschen	Nov. 24 [20], 1820	[April 13, 1819] Died Oct. 9,1854
		Magdalene [Rudel]	Wife	"	July 15, 1820	
		Johann	Son	"	Mar. 25, 1843	
		Hanna	Daughter	"	Dec. 25, 1845	
		Andreas	Son	"	1849	Died Oct. 5, 1854
			Daughter	"	Jan. 10, 1852	
85.	Wenke	Carl Traugott	Cottager	"	April 11, 1812	
		Eleonore	Wife	"	[Dec. 7], 1809	
		Marie	Daughter	"	[Ap. 21], 1841	
		Carl Traugott	Son	"	Dec. 1851	
	Schwartz	Joh. Heinrich	Stepson	"	Mar. 1, 1834	
86.	Bjar [Biar]	Johann	Blacksmith	Gröditz	Feb. 16, 1823	
		Magdalena [Mehle]	Wife	"	Nov. [19], 1825	
		Johann	Son	"	Aug. 30, 1850	
		Andreas	"	"	Oct. 28, 1853	
87.	Wagner	Mattheus	Gardener	Halbendorff on Spree	Feb. 5, 1825	
		Maria [Kschidel]	Wife	"	[Aug] 1825	
		Johann	Son	"	[July] 1849	

No. & Surname	Given Name	Relation		Origin		Birth	Notes
88. Noak [Noack]	Johann	Cottager	Andreas	Wartha G. Guttau	July 11, 1853	1807	
	Johanna [Pietsch]	Wife	"	"	"	[1816]	
	Hanna	Daughter	"	"	"	June 26, 1837	
	Johann	Son	"	"	"	Dec. 15, 1839	
	Maria	Daughter	"	"	"	Mar. 1, 1842	
	Magdalene	"	"	"	"	Aug. 9, 1844	Died Sept. 19, 1854 at Liverpl
	August	Son	"	"	"	June 6, 1847	
	Christiana	Daughter	"	"	"	Sept. 23, 1849	
	Andreas	Son	"	"	"	Jan. 20, 1852	Died Oct. 27, 1854
	Agnes	Daughter	"	"	"	Mar. 26, 1854	Died Oct. 27, 1854
89. Noak [Noack]	Michael	Locksmith	"	"	"	Feb. 19, 1820	
	[Johanna Lehmann]	Wife	"	"	"	[1826]	
	Maria [Handrick]	Wife [married in TX]	"	"	"	Aug. 5, 1839	
	Wilhelmine	Daughter	"	"	"	Mar. 8, 1849	
	Auguste	"	"	"	"	1852	
	August Ernst	Son	"	"	"	Aug. 12, 1854	Died Nov. 19, 1854
	Carl August	Son	"	"	"	July 26, 1857	[Born in Texas]
	Ernst Emil	"	"	"	"	Jan. 11, 1860	"
	Theresia Bertha	Daughter	"	"	"	June 20, 1861	"
	Johann	Son	"	"	"	Feb. 27, 1866	"
	Johann Paul	"	"	"	"	July 19, 1862	"
90. Weise	Carl Benj.	Skilled laborer	"	"	"	Feb. 6, 1820	
	Maria [Noack]	Wife	"	"	"	1812	
	Magdalena	Daughter	"	"	"	[Aug. 13], 1837	
	Carl August	Son	"	"	"	1842	
	Ernstina	Daughter	"	"	"	1850	
	Ernst	Son	"	"	"	June 21, 1854	

No.	Surname	Name	Relation	Date		Origin	Notes
91	Falke	Georg	Gardener	No. 15, 1812	"		
		Agnes [Rudel]	Wife	June 2, 1816	"		
		Johann	Son	Jan. 3, 1837	"		
		Hanna	Daughter	Aug. 2, 1839	"		Died Aug. 15, 1856 at Roundtop
		Ernst	Son	Oct. 11, 1841	"		
		Maria	Daughter	Dec. 15, 1847	"		
		Magdalene	"	Sept. 18, 1854	"		Born on ship; died on ship Sept. 23
92	Buettner	Andreas	Cottager	Feb. 15, 1802	"	Wartha near Guttau	
		Maria Magdale	Daughter	1835	"		
		Carl Aug. Michael	Son	1842	"		
		Agnes	Daughter	1844	"		
		Caroline	"	1847	"		
		Joh. August	Son	1851	"		Died Oct. 19
93	Pampel	Peter	Cottager/cabinetmaker	Jan. 18, 1808	"		
		Agnes [Noack]	Wife	1809	"		Died Sept. 18 [21] at Liverpool
		Hanna	Daughter	1839	"		
		Carl Heinrich	Son	Feb. 7, 1842	"		[Sept. 21, 1854 Liverpool]
		August	"	May 7, 1844	"		
94	Spahn	Johann	Blacksmith	1828	"		
95	Meltschak	Johann	Skilled laborer	July 20, 1815	"	Königswarthe	
		Maria	Wife	May 16, 1805	"	"	
96	Moerbe	Ferdin. Jacob	Tailor & Gardener	Dec. 6, 1828	"	Neudorf near Guttau	
		Anna [Holfeld]	Wife	Dec. 22, 1828	"	"	[communed] Nov. 29 buried Nov. 30

No.	Surname	Given Name	Status	Place	Born	Date	Notes
97.	Schoenig	Johann	Day laborer	Baruth	"	Aug. 26, 1805	
98.	Hantschke	Andreas	Cottager	"	"	March 6, 1794	
		Hanna [Zieschang]	Wife	"	"	Dec. 5, 1818	
99.	Pampel	Michael	Day laborer	Zittau	"	June 18, 1819	
		Joh. Juliana	Wife	"	"	Oct. 30, 1827	
		Gustav Adolph	Son	"	"	Jan. 5, 1853	
100.	Regmann	Johanna	Maid	Wawitz	"	1838	
101.	Dube	Michael	Half-farmer	Rodewitz	"	Sept. 27, 1807	Died Sept. 29 on the ship
		Joh. Rosina [Tanninger]	Wife	"	"	Dec. 18 [15], 1807	
		August	Son	"	"	March 9, 1831	
		Christiana	Daughter	"	"	[Sept. 17], 1832	
		Johanna	"	"	"	[Aug. 4], 1834	
			"			1836	
		Eleanora	Son	"	"	[July 6], 1839	
		Karl	Daughter	"	"	1841 [Dec. 25, 1840]	
		Ernstina	"	"	"	1847	Died Dec. 22 near Houston
		Marie	Son	"	"	Aug. 5 [July 27], 1849	
		Ernst	Daughter	"	"	June 4, 1851	
102.	Rensch	Magdalena	Maid	"	"	1826	
103.	Ritter	Adam	Blacksmith	Rodewitz	"	June 13, 1833	
104.	Ritter [Ritscher]	Agnes	Maid	"	"	[May 21, 1826]	
		Maria	Daughter	"	"	Nov. 25, 1852	Died Oct. 11
105.	Ritter	Anna	Maid	"	"	Oct. 29, 1836	

	Name	Relation	Place	Date	Notes
106. Schlemmer	Andrea	Tailor	"	Sept. 20, 1820	
	Theresia [Polenz]	Wife	"	1827	
	Carl August	Son	"	Mar. 2, 1850	
	Mar. Magdal.	Daughter	"	Sept. 27, 1853	Died Sept. 30 on the ship
107. Pilak	Andreas	Gardener	"	[Dec. 17], 1798	
	Maria [Urban]	Wife	"	1800	
	Magdalena	Daughter	"	[Aug. 15], 1830	
	Maria	"	"	1850	
	Hanna	"	"	1853	[d. Oct 7, 1854 Liverpool]
	[Johann]	[Son]	"	[1834]	
	Andreas	Son	"	[Feb. 10], 1840	
108. Born	Georg	Miller	Crosta near Milkel	Jan. 9, 1826	
	Maria	Wife	"	Nov. 4, 1823	
	Maria	Daughter	"	April 7, 1851	
109. Sommer	Johann	Mason	Quatitz	Aug. 1, 1822	
	Gertraud	Wife	"	1832	
	Joh. Traugott)	Twins	"	June, 1854	
	Joh. Ernst)		"	June, 1854	
110. Sonsel	Hanna	Widow	Lömischau	1805	
	Carl August	Son	"	1833	
	Magdalena	Daughter	"	1837	
	Ernst	Son	"	1840	
	Andreas	"	"	1844	
	Hanna	Daughter	"	1846	

	Name	Role	Place	Region	Date	Notes
111. Pampel	Johann	Landlord	Särchen	"	--[Sept. 1807]	Died Nov. 21, 1854 [Atlantic]
	Agnes [Belas]	Wife	"	"	---	
	Agnes	Daughter	"	"	--- [1840]	
	Joh. Traugott	Son	"	"	---	
	Peter	"	"	"	---[Feb. 16, 1848]	
112. Schneider Nowotonik	Hans	Hired hand	Spreewitz	"	May 24, 1829	
	Magdalena	Fiancee	Zerre	"	May 6, 1834	
113. Wagner	Magdalena	Cottager's daughter	Weigersdorf	Rothenburg	April 16, 1831	
114. Mikan	Michael	Laborer	Gröditz	Saxony	Jan. 21, 1821	Children: Andreas, Anna, Johann, Peter
115. Richter	Carl Ernst	Wheelwright	Viereichen near Reichswalde		Oct. 25, 1831	
116. Magnus	August	Tailor	Leipe	---		(10 Thaler returned to him)
117. Duerrlich	Johann	Hired hand	Weicha	Saxony		Died 1855
118. Handrick	Johann	Gardener	"	"	Oct. 1, 1811	
	Hanna [Schneider]	Wife	"	"	June 14, 1818	
	Maria	Daughter	"	"	Aug. 5, 1839	
	Hanna Christiana	"	"	"	March 11, 1811	
	Johann	Son	"	"	April 8, 1844	
	Maria Magdalena	Daughter	"	"	Sept. 12, 1847	
	Agnes	"	"	"	Nov. 16, 1850	
	Christiana Theresia	"	"	"	Dec. 27, 1853	
119. Jeschke	Joh. Traugott	Cottager	Weicha	"	April 26, 1813	Died Oct. 1
	Hanna	Wife	"	"	Sept. 16, 1811	

No. / Surname	Given name(s)	Relation	Place		Date	Notes
	Maria	Daughter	"	"	Jan. 5, 1846	Died Nov. 12 [Atlantic]
	August)	Twins	"	"	April 4, 1851	Died Sept. 23 in Liverpool
	Johann Ernst)		"	"	April 4, 1851	
120. Fiedler	Carl August	Resident	Görlitz	"	July 9, 1816	
	Johann Christian	Wife	"	"	Aug. 16, 1816	[Line through name]
	Emilie Bertha	Daughter	"	"	May 7, 1844	
	Joh. Carl August	Son	"	"	Nov. 25, 1845	
	Anna Maria	Daughter		"	July 24, 1848	
121. Noack	Johann	Cottager	Gröditz	"	March 1823	
	Magdalena	Wife	"	"	1812	Died Oct. 22
122. Richter	Joh. Gottlieb Ernst	Mason	[Mengelsdorf]	---	Jan. [1819]	[Document frayed]
	Hanna	Wife	---	---	Feb.	
	Simon Johannes	Son	---	---	Nov.	
	August Hermann	Son	---	---	Aug. 22, 1852	Died Nov. 12 [Atlantic]
123. Simmank	Johann Ernst	Cottager	[Carlsbrunn]	"	Jan. 21, 1826	
	Johanna Luise	Wife		"	April 4, 1828	
	Ernst Adolph	Son		"	June 15, 1851	
	Luise Ernstina	Daughter		"	July 11, 1853	
124. Zieschank	Johann	Master miller	[Gross Saubernitz]	"	April 11, 1810	
	Hanna [Hommel]	Wife	---	"	Nov. 25, 1808	
Kasper	Maria	Wife	[Gross Radisch]	"	April 22, 1829	[illegible]
Gruelich	Maria	Her child	---	"	June 13, 1852	Died [Jan. 1855]
125. Tjchornak	Johann	Cottager	[Dürrbach]	"	1814	
	Hanna [Herenz]	Wife	---	"	1819	
	Marie	Daughter	---	"	Jan. 17, 1844	
	Johann	Son	---	"	---	

No.	Surname	Given Name	Relationship	[Place]	Origin	Birth Date	Death/Notes
		Hanna	Daughter	---	"	1847	
		Rosina	"	---	"	Feb. 10, 1850	Died Oct. 8 [Queenstown]
		Agnes	"	---	"	Mar. 13, 1853	Died Oct. 23 [Queenstown]
126.	Mrosko	Matthaus	Cottager	[Dürrbach]	Saxony	April 13, 1814	
		Hanna [Schoellnick]	Wife	"	"	Jan. 1, 1818	
		Maria	Daughter	"	"	Oct. 13, 1837	
		Hanna	"	"	"	Sept. 13, 1840	
		Rosina	"	"	"	Aug. 1, 1843	
		Agnes	"	"	"	June 5, 1849	
		Magdalena	"	"	"	Feb. 8, 1854	
127.	Fritsche [Britsche]	Johann	Cottager & butcher	[Briesing]	"	Feb. 18, 1817	
		Hanna	Wife	---	"	Feb. 18, 1810	
		Magdalena	Daughter	"	"	March 6, 1840	[d. Oct. 5, 1854 Queenstown]
128.	Schneider	Michael	Laborer	[Nechern]	"	April 10, 1812	
		Maria [Kerk]	Wife	---	"	May 1, 1825	
		Magdalena	Daughter	"	"	March 6, 1849	
129.	Kerk	Johann	Gardener	[Dauban]	"	Jan. 6, 1789	
		Agnes	Wife		"	Feb. 2, [1808]	
		Hanna	Daughter		"	Feb. 4, 1823	
		Magdalena	Daughter		"	Jan. 24, [1828]	
		Agnes	"		"	[1831]	
		Johann	Son		"	[1833]	
130.	Tzscho [illegible] [Schoppa]	[Traugott]	[Cottager]	Thiemendorf	—	Dec. 9, 1815	Died [Jan. 4, 1855 at San Felipe]
		[Anna Rosina]	Wife	"	"	Jan. 17, 1814	
		[Karl Traugott]	Son	"	"	Jan. 25, 1835	
		[Friedrich August]	Son	"	"	July 12, 1840	
		[Johanne Ernstine]	Daughter	"	"	Aug. 14, 1846	

	Name	Relation/Occupation	Birthplace		Date	Remarks
	August Heinrich	Son	"	"	June 13, 1851	
131. Dube	Johann	[Mill owner]	Prausske [Cornitz]	"	April 24, 1826	
	Magdalena [Gross]	Wife	"	"	June 22, 1829	
	Carl August	Son	"	"	June 14, 1853	[d. Oct. 12, 1854 Queenstown]
132. Kokel	Christoph	[illegible]	Reichwalde	"	Jan. 14, 1823	
	Maria [Schneider]	Wife	"	"	Nov. 30, 1830	
	Christiana	Daughter	"	"	Aug. 26, 1851	
	Johann	Son	"	"	June 29, 1854	
133. Peter	Matthaus	Retired estate owner	"	"	1789	
	Rosina [Lushiz]	Wife	"	"	1793	
134. Schiwart	Christoph	Cottager	Kl. Radisch	—	Mar. 29, 1825	
	Hanna [Schuster]	Wife	"	"	Dec. 18, 1823	
	Maria	Daughter	"	"	May 22, 1851	
135. Bartel-Merting	Johann	Cottager	Thomaswalde	"	Feb. 9, 1824	Died on the ship [Oct. 4, 1854]
	Hanna [Janetz]	Wife	"	"	Mar. 1826	Died on the ship Sept. 27
	Johann	Son	"	"	Feb. 27, 1851	Died Oct. 11 [Queenstown]
	Matthaus	"	"	"	April 24, 1853	
136. Bartel-Merting	Johann	Retired estate owner	"	"	April 17, 1780	Died aboard ship [Sept. 27, 1854]
	Hanna	Wife	"	"	Sept. 1796	
137. Kruper-Hole	Matthaus)	Brothers	Jahmen	Rothenburg	April 11, 1830	
	Christoph)		"		April 5, 1834	Died Sept. 30 near Queenstown
138. Suchi	Johann	Mill master	Sdier	---	---	

No. & Name	Given Names	Occupation	Place		Birth	Death
139. Pampel	Hanna	Maid	Särchen near Klix	"	---	---
140. Taffel	Bernhard	---	Niedergurig	"	---	---
141. Matke	Hanna Hanna	--- ---	Klitten		Rothenburg May 24, 1816 Oct. 13, 1847	Died [Oct. 4, 1854 Queenst.]
142. Nowak	Johann	---	Lemischau	---	---	
143. Eiffler	Carl Gottlieb		Schöps near Weissenberg---			
144. Scharath	John Gottlieb Johanna [Domann] Wilhelmine Ferdinand Paul	[illegible] [Wife] [Daughter] [Son]	Dauban " " "		Rothenburg Oct. 28, 1805 March [8], 1815 April 11, 1844 [May 8,] 1848	Died April 9, 1855
145. Islet	Rosina [Schuster] Andreas Johann) August) Matthaus)	Cottager's widow " Children	Klitten		--- April 10, 1842 June 8, 1836 July 23, 183[8] Mar. 7, 1847	Died Oct. 15, 1854
146. Lorentschk	Hanna Maria	Unmarried Daughter	Reichwalde "		Rothenburg Dec. 29, 1805 Nov. 28, 1837	Died Oct. 5 [Queenstown]
147. Kolba	Matthaus	Retired estate owner	Neudorf near Spreewitz	---		
148. Casparik	Magdalena	Working woman	Neudorf	"	---	Died Nov. 9 [Atlantic]
149. Schmidt	Joh. Christiane	Maid	Krischa	"	---	

	Given name	Occupation	Place	Region	Date	Notes
150. Werthschutz	Johann	Weaver	Carlsbrunn	"	---	
151. Nowak	Wilhelm	Mill apprentice	Dürrbach	"	Feb. 16, 1824	
152. Nowak	Carl Ernst	Mill apprentice	Gross Saubernitz		Dec. 23, 1833	
153. Noack	Hanna	Maid	Wartha	Saxony	---	
154. Buettner	Maria Magdalena	Maid	"			
155. Wuensche	Christoph	Landlord	Weissenberg	"	June 25, 1812	
	Maria [Wehle]	Wife	"	"	[Feb. 2], 1804	
	Johann August	Son	"	"	Dec. 15, 1837	
	Andreas Traugott	"	"	"	Sept. 20, 1841	
	Johann Ernst	"	"	"	Aug. 29, 1846	Died Oct. 10 [Queenstown]
156. Melde	Andreas	---	Doberschitz	"	Dec. 25, 1825	
157. Trinks	Gottfried	Landlord	Sopienthal near Muskau	"	---	
	Elizabeth	Wife	"		60 years old.	Died Oct. 10 [Queenstown] [Three grown children]
[158] Mieksch	2 persons	Miller	Loebau	Saxony	---	[illegible]
[159] Hiob	[Andreas]	Carpenter	Klix			
[160] [illegible]		Locksmith	Dresden			
[161] Minzlaff		Agricultural Admin.	Dresden			
[162] ---		Butcher	Schoeps			

			Petersdorf	Farmhand	
[163]	—			Farmhand	
[164]	Schuster	[Carl]	Gersdorf, Saxony	Cabinetmaker	
[165]	Haak	[Carl]	Prettisch, Posen	Shoemaker	
[166]	Linak	[Matthaus]	Zerre	Day laborer	
[167]	Birnbaum	Joseph	Oberlichtenwalde		Married on the Inconstant
[168]	Eiffler	Friedrich	Kloch	Farmer	
[169]	Friedrich	Wilhelm	Reichwalde	Weaver	
[170]	Gedlich	G.	Ruppersdorf near Herrnhut		
[171]	Jaeger	Carl	Weissenberg	Mason	
[172]	Jenke	Antoine [Agnes]	Reichwalde	unmarried	
[173]	Jeremias	Johann	Belger	Farmer	
[174]	Kokel	Andreas	Reichwalde	unmarried	
[175]	Kelling	Franz	Dauban	Farmer	
[176]	Merting	George	Thomaswalde	Farmer	
[177]	Müller	Hermann	Seifersdorf, Prussia		

George R. Nielsen

From Kilian's death list in *Serbske Nowiny* and not added to passenger list:

37. Ann Kasper, Grossradisch 1 Day 6 Dec 1854 Atlantic – of Maria
78. Anna Born several days weakness Houston – of George Born
79. Maria Born several days weakness Houston – of George Born
80. Jannasch age: several days Houston

[G. Nielsen]

[1855] Kilian to Walther [Concordia Historical Institute]

This is Kilian's first letter to C. F. W. Walther in which he applied for admission to the church. Decide for yourself if it was a letter to a friend and classmate or if it was to a respected colleague. Walther, also the editor of Der Lutheraner, included segments of the letter in the March 15, 1855 issue.

9 Feb 1855

Dear most reverend Professor and Pastor!

Trusting in your unending effort to represent the church of pure confessions to all parts of the United States, I, as a pastor who recently immigrated into Texas, would like to present you with the following:

It was in the year 1853 when thirty plus Wends, Prussian Lutherans, who left the Prussian national church union and returned to the Evangelical Lutheran Church, emigrated to Texas through Bremen, suffered shipwreck on the Island of Cuba, but escaped with their lives. They wrote favorable letters to their friends during the winter of 1854 so that an association of more than 500 souls followed them. This Evangelical Lutheran congregation, composed of so-called Old Lutheran Prussian families, joined by 200 souls of the Saxon national church, called me as pastor and teacher to accompany them over here. The association was transported by the ship line Valentin Lorenz Meyer through Hamburg and Liverpool. I arrived with this congregation at Galveston on 16 December of last year, and after the poorer families, out of necessity, had found work in Houston and vicinity, I traveled 200 English miles inland with the wealthier ones. Here on Rabbs Creek in Bastrop County that portion of the association yet not divested of wealth, who also paid for the overseas transport of the poorer ones, are in the process of purchasing a league of land so as to enable the poorer ones to come to the new homeland. There is an abundance of uninhabited land around here, but because of the difficulty of finding the rightful owners of the land in Texas, it has not been possible for the people to buy any and so for weeks they have had to live in huts. In general this congregation of mine went through many adversities even though the voyage itself went without a storm. We lost 70 persons during the trip, mostly from cholera which struck while the association crossed England. Several persons already died in Liverpool. Nevertheless, we departed from Liverpool on 26 September on the large English two-decker BEN NEVIS (Captain Herron), besides the ship's personnel, about 580 souls, since besides our private party, other passengers from Germany also went along. During the very calm four-day voyage through the Irish Channel many deaths occurred, one after another, due to cholera, so that we were forced to spend three weeks in quarantine in the harbor of Cork in Ireland. Our overseas voyage to Galveston took seven and one-half weeks. Also during this time several more died.

After this preliminary note please consider also my request, that led me to write this letter. I, a Saxon by birth, was the Lutheran pastor in Kotitz in the Kingdom of Saxony, for eleven years since the 24th of September 1837. Dr. [Wilhelm] Sihler, prior to his journey to America, visited me there. In the fall of 1848 I crossed over into Prussia in the area of Niesky, to serve in the pulpit of an emerging scattered group of so-called Old Lutherans in opposition to the Prussian state church. Even though this scattered congregation, as a result of my moving from Saxony, was elevated as a parish of its own, and I as its pastor was formally recognized by the Prussian government, motives were present among those families who had separated from the Union church, to forsake this particular place and to immigrate. I also found myself in some respects so restricted that I was moved to accept the call of the immigrants. After I arrived with my brethren I heard that all the diplomas and documents that a pastor brings from Germany do not authorize him here in the state to perform marriages, and that it is necessary to be authorized by your synod. Now many are thinking about the necessity of marriage because during the journey husbands lost their wives and even more wives lost their husbands through death. I must therefore, before I can be authorized to perform marriages, perform the marriage union through a justice of the peace or through other pastors who are available. Already two couples in need of a marriage service, during my absence and without my knowledge, have been married by a Methodist pastor. It has also been ordered that I must obtain the eligibility from your synod quickly. I can now, of course, quickly and easily obtain certification from the nearest pastor in Galveston, who is the President of the Texas Synod. I have on my own already noticed so many reformed elements in the Texas Synod, that I cannot be inclined to join with it. I did not fight against the Union in Germany in order to actually acknowledge it now. I also feel a dislike for a church service that is so barren, almost without liturgy, as it here appears. The old Saxon style and manner in which the church service and sacraments are held has gone over into my flesh and blood. And I know that the Missouri Synod upholds for all practical purposes, my churchly concept as I believe, and the book, *Die Stimme unserer Kirche in Frage von Kirche und Amt* Erlangen 1852, [The Voice of Our Church on the Question of Church and Ministry], which lies before me, is a book according to my own heart. So I cannot help but ask that you would issue, in the name of your synod, the necessary authorization in the English language.

Even though I would gladly personally present myself to the Missouri Synod, I cannot now appear in St. Louis for obvious reasons. I also base my request for authorization from your synod on the grounds of my personal acquaintance with Dr. Sihler. Also, I should mention that my association with the Missouri Synod in the next year can only be one of written communication.

May I also request of you that you send me your journal, *Der Luthernaner* so I can keep up with you regularly and possibly also contribute essays for it. However, I would also like the entire volume of the previous year for my information. After that I request that a printed constitution of the Missouri Synod be included, and I would like to have a publication from which I can learn the Methodist confession and what you have written about them. But the description of their fundamentals must be specific and accurate. I have seen during a short residence in this country that I will be dealing with this religious denomination.

Finally, I request that for the present all my letters and publications, which I should receive, be sent to me in care of Mr. Andrew Vetter, blacksmith in Round Top, Fayette Co., Texas. Mail will not reach me here in the solitude of the oak forest along Rabbs Creek where I am living in the house of one of the migrant brothers of 1853 and where the association wants to establish their new home.—

Awaiting a speedy answer, I remain in the Lord with cordial greetings to Dr. Sihler and the right reverend Missouri Synod, etc.
John Kilian, Ev. Luth. Pastor.

P.S. On the last Friday, 11 February, a league of land was purchased on which the association plans to settle.

[Comment by Walther in *Der Lutheraner*: May the Lord bless our dear brothers together with their faithful shepherd, materially and spiritually, and through them the church on our new homeland!]
[trans. Biar and G. Nielsen]

[1855] Kilian to Dutschmann [*Serbske Nowiny* 9-6-1855, pp.180-187]

Andreas Dutschmann was the teacher in Weigersdorf during Kilian's ministry there. Earlier he had been a participant in the formation of the congregation and continued his work after Kilian's departure. Dutschmann, aware of the public curiosity in the Serbin group, permitted the Wendish newspaper to print the letter.

Letter from America from the clergyman Kilian
To Mr. Teacher Dutschmann in Weigersdorf
At Rabbs-Creek Bastrop County in Texas, March 19, 1855
Dear Friend!

Undoubtedly you and my acquaintances have waited a long time for a letter written by my hand, but I did not write earlier before I knew for sure whether or not we would be able to carry out our intention to found a special colony. But now I am able to inform you that part of our congregation, whose money was not entirely used up through large donations for the poor and other large expenses, moved back here under the leadership of the steadfast miller, Korla Wićaz [Lehmann] from Dauban and his friend, the miller Jan Dub [Dube], from Brauske, who together bought a large portion of land for the purpose of settling there. It was not a simple matter to find such a large portion of land, for in Texas it is difficult to find the real owner of large land portions. The government had given large estates to such as had served the state well. But many of these had already died and their properties are under guardianship so that the property can not be sold, or they live at great distances, or are unknown, or some person might falsely step up to claim the land as their own. So it is an easy matter to be cheated and to stand in danger of losing the acquired lands and be ejected should the real owner suddenly appear with the necessary papers and deeds. Because of these very reasons the territory on which the city of Austin is located got into such litigation in its early days. So Wićaz was forced to conduct some difficult investigation that took him up into the government at Austin, before the real owner of the tract they desired could be determined. Finally, he learned that the one who sold the portion of land and who had paid taxes on it was not able to sell it. The real owner had died in Galveston and no one knew if there were the heirs. But should any of these heirs appear within the next 20 years then anyone living on that land could be ejected. Therefore, if it is one's object to purchase land, the books at Austin must be examined closely. Because the proposed land purchase could not be completed, Wićaz discovered and bought a different tract. In the meantime the 25 families lived under clear skies in huts or as they say "in camp"(pronounced kämp). That lasted already six weeks. 1) Korla Wićaz from Dauban, 2) Jan Dub from Brauske, 3) Family Dub from Rodewitz, 4) Lowka [Lowke] from Klein Radisch, 5)Šewc [Schuster] from Förstgen, 6) Lowka from Reichwalde, 7) Domaška-Jurc [Domaschka] from Kaschel, 8) Krupar-Hola [Hohle] from Jahmen, 9) Pjekar (Hofmann) from Jahmen, 10) Iselt from Klitten, 11) Hans Kašpr [Kasper] from Kolpen, 12) Handrik from Weicha, 13) Nowak [Noack] from Gröditz, 14) Bjar [Biar] from Gröditz, 15) August Gröschel from Särka, 16) Wukaš [Wukasch] from Buchwalde near Hoyerswerda, 17) Jan Křižank [Zieschank] from Groß Saubernitz, 18) Kambor from Wunscha, 19) Bartl-Mertynk [Bartel-Merting] from Domschwalde, 20) Familie Šołta [Schulze] from Wunscha, 21) Hokr [Hocker] from Förstgen, 22) Brytscha [Britsche] from Dubrauke, 23) Ernst Adolf Mjerwa [Moerbe] from Klix, 24) Ferdinand Mjerwa from Neudorf, 25) Mikš [Micksh] from Löbau. Polnik from Weigersdorf, with whom I am at present residing, lives one hour away from this camp. All of these families, including Matej and Jurij Selnik [Schoellnick], living 40 English miles away on some rented land, as well as Schmidt from Reichwalde, who is renting 3 English miles away, will own some of the league of land purchased by Wićaz and Dub in mid February. In this week the families listed here will occupy the purchased land of about 4000 acres in area. During the past week the land was measured and 100 acres were set aside for church and school.

Travel costs in Texas were so high, that had all the poor been moved along, no money would have been available for purchase of land. Also, with such numbers piling up here it would have been difficult to provide them with food, for in this year a poor harvest is expected. Finally, we missed the right time to sow the Turkish wheat. Corn may be planted up to the end of March. Under such conditions many poor families remained in Houston. Also Janaš [Jannasch] from Weissenberg finds himself there and supports himself with watch-making. His wife gave birth to a child but it soon died. Janaš, who suffered a cholera attack in Galveston, recovered in the local hospitals and returned to the great comfort of his family to Houston. Many poor families moved 85 English miles inland (5 English miles equal 1 German mile) and either work or rent at *Industry, New Ulm, Frelsburg*, and at other places. What is meant by "renting?" A field is rented for one year and a portion, generally one-third of the crop, goes to the owner of the land. Teinert also is renting in Frelsburg after I led him with much luggage 85 miles inland. The costs for the hauling luggage were high—$2 for every 100 pounds from Houston to New Ulm. We are located 40 miles still farther inland. For my luggage I was forced to pay $120. The heaviest chests containing books and my wagon are still in Houston. We have been hurt by these heavy transportation costs because the of great amount of luggage we brought.

Most of these poor people would like to follow at the end of the year or even earlier, if they save their wages and the renters bring in a good crop. But it is not sure whether or not they will join the colony. Nor is it sure whether more affluent people who might arrive from Europe in the fall would join our colony or prefer to found a new colony with the poor.

In this country people prefer not to live close together because many cattle are raised and that activity calls for much pasturage. For transportation men, women, and children ride horses. Travel with cart or wagon is difficult because the deep rivers and streams have no bridges. Therefore my wagon remains in Houston for sale.—Now I would like to say a few things about my trip from Weigersdorf to here.

After overcoming the hindrances of which you are aware, I traveled with my family on the 13th of September to Hamburg. The others had arrived there already on the 5th of September, and the Grösl [Groeschel] and Mĕrćin [Miertschin] families from Sarka, had arrived on the 11th. The next morning before dawn the steamship took off from Hamburg and arrived at Grimsby, England on the 12th at 8 o'clock in the evening. There they spent the night. Then they traveled by railroad to Liverpool where, because of the cholera, they were held up until the 26th of September. The Grösl and Mĕrćin families as well as Madlena Sonsel (unmarried) arrived there on the 16th of September. My family and I traveled day and night by train and arrived at Hamburg on the 14th of September. From Hamburg we traveled through Cologne, Ostende, Dover, London to Liverpool because were told that by going this way we would be able to join the others the soonest at Liverpool. Following the advice of Agent Behn I left my luggage at Hamburg. The agent had promised to send it later, but none has arrived yet. So I went from Hamburg to Cologne and from there farther to Ghent, through Aachen and reached Verviers, the Belgian custom-house, where our luggage was examined. In the rush I discovered that my pass had not been returned to me just as the locomotive began to move. Then in the evening in Mecheln there was such a crowd that I barely reached the car leaving for Ghent. I called to my wife to leave her seat in the car because it was going to Brussels. She did not hear and remained seated. The rail agent had not understood her for there French is spoken. I believed that she, together with my little son Gerhard and Hana were in a car destined for Ghent and I rushed for a car going in that direction. So it happened that I traveled to Ghent but my family went to Brussels. I arrived at the city of Ghent in the evening and after stepping off I watched closely if my wife would do likewise, but I saw nothing of her. At the railway station I finally met a Flemish [Dutch-German] person who directed me to the inn, "hotel des Hollande". There I spent a night worrying how my wife and son might be doing. The next morning I sent the aforementioned Flem to the station to seek my wife. He returned that same day with her, having found her in Antwerp where other German emigrants had taken her and helped her find a place to stay. In the meantime I was having my trouble with the police in Ghent who found it very difficult to believe how anyone could possibility could lose a wife and travel pass at the same time. Finally they sent written inquiry to the custom house at Verviers, and after a few days my pass arrived and I could travel on. In an attempt to regain lost time, and to arrive earlier at Liverpool I planned to travel through Ostende, but again I was delayed so that it was the 20th of September when I arrived at Liverpool.

From Ostende the steamship left for Dover towards evening. The sea was rough. In the 2nd class cabin, where we were assigned, there were some people suffering from sea-sickness. At 2 o'clock that night we arrived at Dover. From there my family and I traveled through London and other cities to Liverpool. There, at the cost of Agent Meyer, our group was quartered in three homes. We could not continue because some more had died of cholera.

Finally on the 26th of September we left Liverpool, leaving the sick behind in the Liverpool hospitals. Several who recovered later followed us to Queenstown. In the Irish Channel the weather was peaceful. Now since many passengers took sick with cholera, Captain Herron did not dare to continue, but instead entered the port of Queenstown, Ireland. There the healthy emigrants were loaded on the old frigate "The Inconstant." The sick remained on our old ship "Ben Nevis" until the ship "Elisa," which had been retired, could be outfitted as a hospital. The English physician, Blennerhassel, who was assigned to us died already on the 30th of September. Even though he was Reformed he demanded that I grant him the bounty of Holy Communion and he received it out of consideration of his plight. On the order of the government the physician Dr. Scott visited us, and the German physician Dr. Hanka whom Meyer had sent us, served on the "Inconstant" and also on the "Elisa". Later Dr. Kelly was assigned to us as the journey continued. The featherbeds and furs of the dead and those who took sick were cast overboard or burned. So we spent three weeks under quarantine near Queenstown, where agent Meyer arrived and provided those who had lost bedding with new covers, but featherbeds were outlawed. During the quarantine the owner of the "Ben Nevis" suffered a loss of 1300 Pound Sterling. We had no other expenses beside those we paid ourselves. The English ship crews treated us well but of the Irish that can not be said. My wife and I were spared of the cholera. When cholera quit, measles broke out among many children.

We left Queenstown on October 23. A strong wind arose which caused many to suffer from sea-sickness and at night the luggage and chests were tumbled about and mixed up so that many emigrants lived in fear. Several days later the weather calmed a bit, but when we neared the Azores the wind began again. As the island of St. Maico came in view, conditions improved, but progress slowed until we passed the British isle of Antigua on the right and the French isle of Guadalupe on the left. Then we passed the British isle of Montserrat and as we reached Santo Domingo or Haiti the weather became so calm for three days that the ship just lay still and we suffered from intense heat. Again the wind arose and we passed the isle Grand Cayman, then the isle Cuba. Entering the Gulf of Mexico we approached, after a long time, the Island of Galveston. There a contrary wind held us for five days until December 15 when we reached the sand bar to Galveston, a shallow bay that the larger ships could not enter. Our ship, the "Ben Nevis" was among the larger ones which offered some comfort, but the kitchen was not furnished for such a large number of people and there were other inconveniences. In general our voyage would have succeeded well had it not been for the cholera. Violent storms we did not suffer. The steamship: "Arctic" which left Liverpool about the same time as we collided with a French ship in a fog as it neared New York and sank with a heavy loss of life. That disaster and many other shipwrecks cause us to say that the mercy of God brought us safely to Galveston. When the weather was calm and no one suffered from cholera we held our church services and evening devotions with songs.

On the 15th of December our captain went by boat to Galveston to order a steamer that would transport us and our luggage over the sand bar into the city. This steamer arrived in late forenoon and the emigrants were forced to hurry to get on board with their luggage.

That caused quite a stir but fortunately nothing harmful happened. On the morning of December 16 we entered Galveston. My family and I went to a hotel while many remained on board until the luggage was brought to shore. As I arrived in the morning the place was full of chests and trunks and the customs collectors were checking to see if we had anything to tax. They soon tired of it, we paid $50 and by afternoon we were all on board a steamship with luggage and by evening on the way to Houston. Houston lies inland 80 miles from Galveston. Each one paid one and a half dollars for the trip. One dollar equals 1 Taler and 12 Neugroschen. Even though 81 had died on the voyage still 500 people were on deck as "Ben Nevis" arrived in America. Not all of these could be taken on board the steamship. Therefore our wagons and a large number of emigrants remained in Galveston but would follow us next Thursday. So everything was aground in Houston under the clear sky and a week passed by before the trip inland could be made. I stayed with the Lutheran Pastor Braun in Houston and concerned myself about the emigrants as well as I could. Many poor families, because of the lack of money, remained in Houston where they sought work until they could follow later if they desired to do so. Neumann from Weigersdorf and Jan Greulich from Gebelzig and others remained in Houston (pronounced Hooston). There the watchmaker Janaš made his livelihood. Rychtar [Richter] from Mengelsdorf is also there. Hubran [Urban] from Rackel, whose wife gave birth here, bought land here and will follow. His brother-in-law Wagner from Halbendorf will also follow.

I and my family along with the families Grösl, Teinert, Kerk from Dauban, Kubica [Kubitz] from Dubrauke and Arldt from Weigersdorf had a chance at the weekend to reach New-Ulm. New-Ulm is located 85 English miles from Houston. We had to pay $2 for every hundred pounds of baggage and we had 8300 pounds on two wagons. Ten oxen were hitched to each vehicle. From Houston to the River Brazos we walked across wide prairies, which means meadows, often soggy and wet. The way was miserable, but not once did any wagon upset. We made these 85 English miles (17 German miles) in 15 days. Everybody, except my wife and small children, had to walk. At evening bedspreads were stretched out as tents, feather beds brought in and a fire was made near by for heat and cooking. In rainy weather we found ourselves in uncomfortable condition on the prairie. We had to suffer only a few bad days before we reached the other bank of the Brazos. This was on the third and fourth of January. We had to spend the night there in the prairie because the river had been flooded. It was hard to find a dry spot. The others remained there, but I, my wife, and Gerhard, both of whom I had to carry across a brook, returned to the banks of the Brazos where we found an inn. But that place was overfilled and we were not admitted. We were forced to seek shelter from the cold and wet under a leaky roof where we sat out the night. Next morning we returned to our people but had to wade through water. Finally and fortunately we reached New-Ulm where we had to pay $167 for the transport of our luggage.

We received lodging at a farm which was so overflowing with emigrants that we could not remain and were forced to seek a better place. Another reason for moving was that the delivery time for my wife was not far away. The home of the emigrant Matica [Matthiez] from Kaschel and the home of Domaška-Janak from Reichwald were also overfilled. So I decided to leave New-Ulm and go to my friends at Rabbs creek (pronounced Räbbskrik). So we traveled there and stopped at the house of Polnik from Weigersdorf, 40 miles farther inland from New-Ulm. In the vicinity some of the wealthier people had already bought a portion of land. There in Polnik's house, which he does not own, I live and there my wife gave birth to a daughter on the 13th of February. Maria Theresia was baptized and died on March 14. On March 17 she was buried on that newly acquired land and with her little body the cemetery, which had been dedicated by me, was used for the first time. My wife is in good health.

As far as our meals are concerned we bake corn bread in an iron kettle with lid, with yeast or without, as each desires. We must grind the corn with hand-mills because other mills are too distant.

The Sorbs who migrated earlier are alive and in good health.

What will happen to us, I cannot say at this time. The final design of our colony has not yet been developed so it is difficult to predict with precision. After two or three years one might be able to tell but not now.

Therefore I ask that this letter and the enclosed register of the deceased be passed on to Sir Vicedirector Wanak and to the editor of the *Serbske Nowiny* with the wish that it be made public.

Because I have heard that several of farmers have intended to write hostile letters to Bautzen because of us, so I ask the friends Wanak, Smoler etc. to send me a copy (Note: It will happen [ed.]) so that I might be able to expound on the assertions of my opponents. I notice that I will have opposition here just as I had in the old fatherland. Yet I hope to find comfort here.

Jan Kilian Pastor

[trans Musiat; W. Nielsen]

[1872] Kilian to Smoler [Concordia Historical Institute]

Jan Smoler was a leader in the Sorbian national movement and editor of the Wendish newspaper. The letter, a portion of which is printed here, shows how deeply Kilian was attached to his homeland and the Wendish language.

In Serbin, August 22, 1872
To Mr. J. E. Smoler in Bautzen!
Dear Sir,

For a long time I have not written to you. But recently a copy of the *Łužiski Serbski Słownik* Lusatian Wendish Dictionary, published in 1866, came into my hand. So my heart constrained me to write to Dr. Pfuhl. But I would also, with a small note make some observations to you and request that you send the enclosed letter to Dr. Pfuhl. I find it odd that I first learned of this dictionary and that no one informed me of such a noteworthy appearance of things Sorbian. My old friends Imiš, Wanak and others appear to have assumed that I had become lost in my Texas oak forest, or even have died. Otherwise they surely would have written.

Many words that I come across in the dictionary, or those not in it remind me of the old times that I experienced in the Sorbian area. How gladly would I go for a stroll in the Döhlen Hills, be with my relatives and my Hochkirch, my lovely Kotitz parsonage, as well as the Weigersdorf vegetation and see other things, before my eyes close in death!

My oldest son Gerhard, after five years of training will now become my teacher. So I no longer need to spend time in the schoolroom, but use it to indulge in memories of the land of the Sorbs. We are now provided with three clergymen, two from the Grosspostwich congregation and one from Maltitz. Also I could now move back to the Sorbian area in case anyone would like to have me, and if I could be sure the dear souls I have here [illegible]. So you can surmise that I concern myself with the fortune and welfare of things Sorbian. In Serbin we have brought together Sorbs from the hills [southern Lusatia] and from the heath [central Lusatia].

I have begun to examine your dictionary with great attention, and am ready to take on "B" and "C". In case when an additional word entered my mind, I checked if you have included it. I am making annotations to your book based on my own collections and memories. I encountered many words that I never perceived among the population, just as I miss many words I know that are spoken by the people. Why is that? I assume that your words originate out of the Bautzen and Catholic regions. I, however, have spent my life in an entirely different district than those who with and under you have gathered words for your dictionary. I was born in Döhlen, lived at home for ten years of my life, then 3 years at Hochkirch with my grandfather, from 1837 served as the clergyman in Kotitz for 11 years, and from 1848 on for 6 years in Weigersdorf and Klitten where I cared for several neighboring parishes in Muskau, Spremberg, Cottbus, Burg/Spreewald and Lübben. So I covered much of the land of the Sorbs. However, what concerns the Sorbian pronunciation, Reichwald, for example, where one does not pronounce the "e" but exclusively a clear "l"; neither do they sound a "w": Ja sym najedl, lowa mje boli and so on. It is true that you also have all kinds of my words. But amazingly you fail to include some widely known words as nekrasnik, the unkind, zunčeć, to hum or buzz, (čoly zunča) zabalić, wrap, prjezdsić fiesten, used when speaking of fire, (wohen prjezdsi), skušować, listen, wokoło wójcować, roam about, walni bale, rozprasnyć, beat asunder, burst, rozpraskować, smash and so on...But through clergymen and teachers such names could be gathered, which would take some labor. Also old Sorbian family names should be gathered: Fóžan, Bowš, Dobruša, Bartuš, Losač, Kobanja, Sokowa, Nabuka (farmstead Nabuks in Waditz), Tolšin, Husla, Mikliš, Kubaš, Habač, Nučan, Natužanski, Makowski, Rabowski in Döhlen.

Also it would be worth while to collect Sorbian proverbs. I have gathered three short pages of them, many according to the German pattern....

I would like to mention that the silent "h" at the end of a syllable is not distinguished from the "h" that is sounded. Would perhaps the Greek "spiritus asper" come in handy? Would it not be possible to write bahno, kohlica, prudło, (bryda), cyhlje, nahły and so forth. And how would a stranger know that one does not sound the "h" with čahnyć, sahnyć, prahnyć,

Now this before I close. May I offer an addition to your dictionary? But you must grant me one year's time. In between we must diligently communicate with each other. You represent one-half of the Sorbs and I the other half. Would you or would you not work with me?

As for spelling I find myself at home with it, and is suitable for the learned but not for the unlearned. My supplement to your dictionary would be done according to your orthography, which I hope to master soon. Since I am not yet in control of it and this letter has been written in the old form. Please write right soon either in the mode of the learned or as common people speak. It is all the same to me, just so you write to me. But when I pick up the pen, I begin to make mistakes.

In the hope that my promised additions will not be unwelcome to you I remain,

    Your humble
    Jan Kilian
[trans. W. Nielsen]

[1872] Kilian to Mattig [Concordia Historical Institute]

Kilian not only corresponded with associates and friends in Germany, but with members of his extended family. This letter illustrates Kilian's total immersion in the religious controversy. The letter is to a relative, yet there is little information about the family matters. It also provides us with a sense of how Kilian viewed the conditions.

In Serbin in Texas, 23 August 1872
To: K. A. Mattig, Miller in Uhyst
Dear Uncle,

I received your son Ernst's letter of 5 January this year, in due order. But until now I was unable to find time for an answer, because in each year including this year, storms and hate prevailed in my congregation.

You have recently heard accurately, that in 1870 my congregation split anew, after it had been unified in 1867. The first division was in 1858 due to the conventicles. But the second division originated because of things German, from the very members of my congregation who felt themselves drawn to the German. Serbin is a Wendish colony. We had only one German widow when the colony was founded. But in 1868 we obtained a German teacher for the children. Soon several of our distinguished Sorbs joined with him and with our handful of resident Germans who had settled here, because they had become mixed with the Sorbs through marriage—they wanted to be like the Germans. Misery resulted from such confusion so that a good third of my congregation broke off from me and my Wendish majority in 1870.

One German is one German and a Wend is nothing. This new congregation, that was set up for things German has called a clergyman, J. Pallmer, born in Bederwitz, and has built a new church and parsonage, opposite me that stares me in the face.

But those Wends, who merely rode with the storm whose leaders did not anticipate, that several are now reconsidering, because they do not hear a Wendish sermon on all Sundays, only Wendish and German on alternate weeks. I however, preach Wendish and German all Sundays, because I have several Germans those who felt separation as senseless. Even though, however, our Synod holds one faith for the two congregations, I do not readmit those Wends from

Pallmer's congregation if they wish to rejoin. So the battle begins anew.

Last year we have completed the construction of our new church. It is built out of stone—70 feet long, 40 feet wide and 24 feet high to the roof. The walls are whitewashed inside and outside. Inside the church is painted white and furnished with lovely altar adornments. On the west side is the whitewashed tower with a green roof. We dedicated the building on the first Sunday in Advent and since then I have preached in it. Our old wooden church, where I had preached before, has been completely remodeled and rebuilt for a school

This year in July my oldest son Gerhard returned home from the teachers seminary at Addison where he was trained for five years as a teacher. I had to pay approximately a thousand dollars for it. He has been named as the organist and teacher of my church congregation and I will induct him the next Sunday in eight days. So it will not be necessary for me to teach the children by myself as it has been. So I now anticipate, if God wills it, a better time than before.

And yet I would like to move back to the Sorb area, because here I feel constantly a stranger. In the vicinity we now have three Wendish clergymen, who could replace me—J. Pallmer from Bederwitz, of whom I have already spoken. J. [Andreas] Schmid from Eulowitz and J. Proft from Maltitz so that your son Ernst could also move here, if only I know if he had remained Lutheran or if his Professor Kahnis in Leipzig has not misled him. But I would rather not say more this time. Send the enclosed letter to your son in Annaberg.

[trans. Musiat; G. Nielsen]

[1872] Kilian to Bünger [CHI]

While many Wends, especially those in Australia, generously contributed to Wendish institutions and causes in the homeland, Texas Wends did not. Money they collected was kept in their own congregation or sent to the Lutheran institutions in the United States. In the letter, Kilian also wrote about his friend, Caspar Braun. He often explained a person's disposition or philosophy on the basis of

geography whether they be Saxon, Prussian, Hermannsburger, or
Wuertemberger.

Serbin, Texas 21 October 1872

Rev. T. F. Bünger, St. Louis, Mo.

Reverend Sir, dear President!

Enclosed is a notice of a draft in the amount of $196 in Gold, which will soon reach you; a report and an introduction.

Specification of payments.

For the Building Fund to construct the Evangelical Lutheran Orphanage in St. Louis:

a. From Pastor Pallmer's congregation---------$33.25

b. From Pastor Zimmerman's congreation------ 35.60

c. From Pastor Proft's congregation------------- 15.00

d. From Kilian's congregation-------------------- 34.00

Total---$117.85

Pastor Pallmer's congregation:

For the Synodical Treasury --------------------- 25.00)

For the institute of Pastor Brunn---------------- 3.75) (Delivery note)

Grand Total-------------------------------------$146.60

From the overage of the draft please pay my debts to L. Lange and Barthel. If there is something left over utilize it at your discretion.

Report. Yesterday I ended the meeting of the Missourians in Texas with a divine service by a sermon on Ephesians 4: 1-17, the text requested by the brethren, and Holy Communion in my St. Paul's Church. It was the first Pastoral Conference of Missourians in Texas which took place in 7 sessions in Serbin beginning on October 16. The sessions were held in the stone St. Paul's Church and attended by the pastors J. Pallmer, J. Proft, J. Zimmermann, A. Greif, P. Klindworth, A. Schmidt, J. Kilian (senior), and G. Kilian (junior). Pastor Braun was invited by Pastor Pallmer and me but declined to come. At first I had no real desire for a pastoral conference because of the concerns of which I will relate later. But the conference was splendid! We Missourian ministers thereby melded into a cluster which the devil will not so easily break up. The first three sessions were devoted to homiletical discussions and exercises, and led to a decision based on an idea by Pastor Proft to have smaller circles to

131

meet on each Friday before the full moon and discuss the upcoming sermon texts for the month. The upper circle is composed of Pastor Pallmer, Pastor Proft and Pastor Kilian (senior); the lower circle, Pastor Zimmermann, Pastor Schmidt, Pastor Greif and P. Klindworth.

During the following three sessions Pietism was discussed. The discussion of the theme was chiefly of a church historical nature and was based on the 4 books by J. Arndt *vom wahren Christenthums* [True Christianity]. On Saturday before noon of the seventh session the minutes were discussed which the elected secretary, Pastor Greif, composed with great care, but in part was too lengthy. I was opposed to my taking over the chairmanship because of it I would not be able to freely express myself. But I was told that as president I could speak on matters at hand as much as I wanted to. As chairman I asked Secretary Greif to prepare an abstract of the minutes to send to you. But I wanted to see his abstract before he sent it. That service the versatile and eager-to-learn pastor was glad to do.

We put the young pastors under some pressure when we asked them to preach. But this resistance was overcome when Pastor Schmidt preached the Wendish sermon before noon and Pastor Greif preached the German sermon in the afternoon. Pastor Klindworth preached the German sermon in St. Peter's church for Pastor Pallmer and I announced this in my congregation, to the Wends as well as the Germans. I also went there with my family, to where my worst opponents were with a friendly smile and listened to Pastor Klindworth preach on the Gospel Lesson John 4: 47-54. All three sermons pleased me very much. During the conference we thoroughly discussed the Epistle Lesson Ephesians 6: 10-17 (This year I am preaching on the Epistle Lessons) and I had to study the commentary of von Harless during the stimulating meetings during these days.

Presentation. On September 1 of this year I installed my son Gerhard August Kilian as organist and schoolteacher of St. Paul's Church. A condensation of the message for the installation, which I prepared for you and Director Lindemann, is enclosed. My son is performing well. He plays the organ so well that I must express my satisfaction with the teaching of music at the seminary in Addison. Especially do I like how Gerhard plays the pedals.

However, the placement of my son has given the inducement of an extremely sad disturbance in my mostly Wendish St. Paul's congregation. Carl Teinert feels aggrieved because he is no longer playing the organ which he did by my side in Prussia and over here for over 20 years. He also ran into a very strained relationship and is now making his significant beginning of a new split in the church. The outer sign of this split is his new school, which they started 12 miles from here. It could happen that a [large] portion of the Wendish part of my congregation will not only separate themselves from me, but also from the Missouri Synod.

On the other hand the attitude of Pallmer's congregation became so friendly toward me that a large part of them want to unite with me and my congregation. Thereby I came into a very difficult situation with Pastor Pallmer. So a part of the Serbin residents want to come to me while the another was to go away from me. This brings me to a point of apparent desperation. Therefore look for a place for me in the north, so that I may know where to go should I be compelled to leave Serbin.

However, in my humble opinion I see a way all this can be settled. So that his congregation will no longer be hindered from uniting with my people by his presence, why not call pastor Pallmer away from here? Pastor Pallmer is in a situation where his long stay in Serbin is no longer desirable. And then may the discontented part of my congregation find a pastor, who as my diaconate makes a "New Start," that's how we call the place where the discontented people serve as a good schoolmaster. I do not want to say any more, but await further advice.

It appears that there is some big difficulty in my relations with Pastor Braun beginning to surface. I have established an intimate relationship with him and his family. My Old Adam is satisfied with the respect he has for me. But he is a Wuertemberger and I am a Saxon. The difference between us is so small that both of us avoid referring to it. Furthermore, he is full of missionary zeal for Missouri and now has two more vacancies around Houston, which he wants to fill with Missourians. He also wants to join the Missouri Synod, but had some misunderstanding with people in New Orleans. Because he does not have a sponsor I want to recommend him to the Praesidium in

St. Louis, although I myself have little contact with them. But I tell you, with such candid people like the both of us, Braun and me, the Missouri Synod has the better of it instead of some secret intriguers. It appears to me that it is too hard for Pastor Braun to have to go to St. Louis to receive the desired colloquy. Perhaps a way may be found that a man from St. Louis could hold the colloquy in Pastor Braun's home in Houston. A pastor from New Orleans, as well as I, may not be suitable for this. I am too close to Pastor Braun to do this. A pastor from New Orleans is not suited because he does not get along too well with him. Therefore, I ask that Pastor Braun be treated cautiously.

This letter has some very delicate items. That is why you must deal with the contents *interioris admissionsis*. I make my position known with the words of Paul: "As unknown, and yet well known; as dying, and, behold, we live," etc. I place my confidence in God, and remain in the Lord.

Yours faithfully,
Johann Kilian, Pastor

[trans. Biar]

[1872] Kilian to Teinert [Blasig Collection]

The friendship between Kilian and Teinert had existed for more than twenty years and went back to the days when Teinert and Kilian visited the outlying clusters of the Weigersdorf parish. But even such a close friendship had become strained. The letter to Teinert shows the human side of Kilian, receiving sensible advice from his wife and attempting to act on it in a formal manner.

Copy   Serbin 21 December 1872
To Carl Teinert Serbin
Dear Teinert!

My wife and Gerhard are at Giddings today. I am therefore by my self. My wife and Gerhard urge me that I should reconcile myself with you. But how will I begin? It occurred to me that I should write a letter to you.

When I reflect on it all, I must say that I have wronged you as you have me. And you have wronged me as much as I did you. What has happened should be forgotten.

We should unite ourselves in the prayer of the tax collector "God be merciful to me a sinner." Grace can and will unite us, nothing else.

The Pallmer congregation has brought me unrest; that I anticipated a long time. Therefore I would like make peace with you. Come to me without hesitation as freely and often as you wish. Just do not dwell on the past. That would upset me again.

This is enough to clarify my position on reconciliation with you.

I remain in love.

Sincerely, Johann Kilian, P.

[trans. G. Nielsen]

[1873] Kilian to Zimmerman [Blasig Collection]

Frailty and death are common denominators. This letter contains an account of how Kilian and Pallmer, both Wends and neighbors, but pastors in competing congregations, resolved matters of separation.

Serbin 3 September 1873

The Rev. J. Zimmermann, Spring Creek
Dear brother in the ministry,

With the enclosed notice you are receiving the news that our brother Pastor Pallmer departed this world on the morning of September 1 at 11 o'clock. He went home during the peals of the bell. He fell asleep just at the time as the ringing began in our St. Paul church, because it was honoring the approach of a funeral procession. After the death of his wife on July 4 he became very sick, although after several attacks of fever he recovered. He again carried on, preached and participated in a special conference. We both, I and he, were called by Pastor Proft to the West Yegua to resolve an emerging conflict between the pastor and the congregation. I did not go because of my ill health, so he carried out the mission himself. On the evening of August 20 he visited me and told me that he had brought everything concerning his deceased wife to order. That greatly affected him and he believed he would again become ill. And truly he became sick on August 21. I saw him for the last time on August 26. Because on August 27 I myself contracted a very severe attack of fever. Good medical care deflected a second attack, but I was so weak that I could do nothing and could not go out. But I did write letters when necessary. So it happened that on September 2 the fellow pastor of Pallmer, Pastor Proft, performed the burial in the name of both congregations.

May I say a bit concerning my relationship with Pastor Pallmer. Both of us from the beginning of our acquaintance basically were drawn into opposition. Except we were one in our theological starting point. I stand on justification by faith and am therefore opposed to all pietism. That is how Pastor Pallmer stood. But in Serbin he always suffered much from the mutual enmity of both parties and both congregations. We could not become intimate with each other, but had to limit our conduct, each because of his people. In recent times the distance between us both was bridged. A somewhat domineering personality was Pallmer's weak side. But his wife died on July 4 and I buried her at his request. This event removed all empty shadows. We became the most intimate of friends and visited each other often. An absolutely beautiful morning dawned and promised a bright day. The fact that both congregations stood there divided did not prevent us any more. Except death came and destroyed everything. The youthful vigorous man faded unexpectedly and sank into his grave. I, a 62 year old pilgrim, remain and mourn my friend who left too early. Up there all will be made clear.

Enough. God's faithful protection remain over you and your wife and your,

Johann Kilian, P.

[trans. G. Nielsen]

[1876] Kilian to Hermann [Blasig Collection]

*Kilian, the loving father, wrote many letters to his son during his
studies in Indiana. Here is one that serves as an example.*

Serbin, Lee Co. Texas 29 May 1876
To Hermann Theodore, Fort Wayne.
My dear Hermann!

I must answer your letter of May 13. On May 14, I installed
Pastor Geyer at St. Peter's congregation at the instruction of President
Biltz, and with the assistance of pastors J. Zimmerman and T.
Stiemke. Nothing came of the unification of both congregations in
Serbin. The prayer of our Savior in John 17, 20: 2- 23 will not be
fulfilled in Serbin. The old antagonisms remain. Yet I have taken it
upon myself to be friendly with Pastor Geyer as long as possible.

As you are about to begin your vacation I will announce my wish
that you come home if it is possible. We would like to see you. Only
I do not know how much money you have in your cash box and how
much travel money I need to send you. Also, when you want to come
and do you want to take the chance of traveling here alone? Write to
me immediately how much money you need. Talk about it with
Professor Bischoff.

When I think about you being fearful of the fourth year because
you will begin the study of Greek, I suggest that you bring along the
Greek Grammar which Fort Wayne has adopted. Then during your
vacation you can learn the Greek alphabet and read Greek with me
without great effort. There will be enough time left over for
relaxation and visiting. Also bring your wardrobe along so it, where
necessary, can be organized and enlarged.

It is true that we had many weddings and baptisms in the
beginning of the year. But now we have entered a time where no
child has been born and no one died. Only private communions did I
have one after the other. In such cases your brother Gerhard took me
there in our new carriage. You may also drive in it when, God
willing, you come here.

The conference, which we clergymen held from April 21 to 27 at
William Penn near the Brazos, brought me pleasure even though as

the elected president, I had much to do. Pastor Klindworth is a pleasant person and so is his wife.

We are all healthy. Your mother sends her hearty greetings and rejoices in the hope that she will see you. Your siblings also send friendly greetings.

So much for today. More when we can talk. Remain in the Lord's protection. I remain with your mother and siblings in the Lord. Your loving father,
Johann Kilian, P.
[trans. G. Nielsen; Biar]

NOTES

Abbreviations for sources of letters: Concordia Historical Institute, St. Louis, Missouri (CHI); Texas Wendish Heritage Society, Serbin, Texas (TWHS); *Trinitatusgemeinde*, Weigersdorf, Germany (W).

Chapter I – Kilian in Europe 1811-1854

1. Kilian to Jan Smoler, 22 August 1872 (CHI); Kilian to C. F. W. Walther, February 1873 (CHI).

2. George R. Nielsen, *In Search of a Home: Nineteenth-Century Wendish Immigration* (College Station, Texas: Texas A & M University Press, 1989), 4, 5. Because the biography is intended primarily for American readers, the more familiar term Wends will be used instead of Sorbs, and Johann Kilian instead of Jan Kilian.

3. Jan Šołta, *Geschichte der Sorben* (Bautzen, Germany: VEB Domowina - Verlag, 1973), vol. 3; 31, 59.

4. Arnd Matthes, "Kindheit eines Auswanderers," *Oberlausitzer Hausbuch 1998*, 164-165; Kilian to Gottfried Fritschel, 26 January 1880, Wartburg Seminary, Dubuque, Iowa. Döhlen and Niethen were villages that belonged to the Hochkirch parish.

5. Peter Kunze, *Jan Arnošt Smoler: Ein Leben für sein Volk* (Bautzen: Domowina-Verlag, 1995) 16.

6. Kunze, 16.

7. Kunze, 15-17.

8. "Nomina Inscriptorum Tectore per Semestre aeftinum Anni 1819," University of Leipzig Archives; Kilian to Walther February 1873; Richter, or Rychtar, also a Wend, eventually occupied the pulpit at Kotitz and carried on a correspondence with Kilian. He also was interested in millennialism. Šołta, 70, 71.

9. Gerald Stone, *The Smallest Slavonic Nation: The Sorbs of Lusatia* (London: The Athlone Press, 1972) 52-3. C. F. W. Walther said there were only three faculty members who were not "coarse rationalists." Walter O. Forester, *Zion on the Mississippi: The Settlement of the Saxon Lutherans in Missouri, 1839-1841* (St. Louis: Concordia Publishing House, 1953), 25. Walther joined the Pietistic circle. Peter Hauptmann, "Das Konkordienbuch für die Obersorben," *Lutherische Theologie und Kirche*, 1994, 116.

10. Kilian to Adolph Harless, 24 November 1851 (W); Arnošt Wjezar "Serbsk kolonija w. Texasu a jeje wjednik Jan Kilian," *Lužica* 1930.

11. Kotitz Files in Weissenberg Church Archives. Kilian was ordained by Pastor Jakub.

12. Mary help us in our need through your son's bitter death.

13. *Budissiner Nachrichten* 20 April 1854; *Die Oberlaustiz als besondere Abteilung von Sachsens Kirchen- Galerie* (Dresden: Verlag von Hermann Schmidt, ca.1840), 176, 285-292; S. H. Wiedmer to Bill Biar, 19 July 1971, (In author's possession).

14. Kilian added a number of prayers to the Frensius book on the Lord's Supper, and it was one of the books some immigrants such as Wuchatsch took along to Australia. Hauptmann 101. Several books were popular enough to justify new editions.

15. Trudla Malinkowa, *Ufer der Hoffnung* (Bautzen, Germany: Domowina-Verlag, 2nd. edition, 1999), 108.

16. Malinkowa 108.

17. Stone, 19; Šołta, 96.

18. Stone, 148; Šołta, 110.

19. Malinkowa, 108.

20. Nielsen, 67.

21. *Budissiner Nachrichten*, 31 December 1845; Kilian to J. C. W. Lindemann, 11 April 1867 (CHI); Malinkowa, 108.

22. Malinkowa, 109; After a meeting of 900 teachers at Dresden in 1848, Kilian suspected another attempt at separating the schools from the church and wrote another petition. The editor of the Bautzen journal, *Der Erzähler an der Spree* printed the petition, labeled it false, and disputed it point-by point. 27 October 1848, 343-345.

23. Johann Kilian, *Die nothwendige Vorsicht lutherischer Christen bei jetziger Glaubensverwirrung: Ein ernstes Wort an das evangelische Volk, in wendischer Sprache herausgegeben* (Leipzig: Karl Friedrich Dörffling, 1846); *Der Lutheraner*, 13 March 1855, 117-118; Kilian to Walther, 9 February 1855 (CHI).

24. Kilian to Harless, 24 November 1851.

25. Malinkowa, 110.

26. Malinkowa 110; Kilian to Harless, 24 November 1851.

27. Walter J. Rauch, *Presse und Volkstum der Lausitzer Sorben* (Würzburg: Holzner-Verlag, 1959), 103-4. Rauch stated that Kilian sympathized with the Hermannsburger Free Church. Later in Texas Kilian found fault with Pastor Andreas Schmidt who was influenced by the Hermannsburg philosophy. Kilian to J. F. Bünger 22 June 1871 (CHI); Kilian to Kreisdirection, 23 August 1847 (W); Kilian to Harless, 24 November 1851; Hauptmann, 115.

28. The Moravian Brethren and Pietism were both reactions to the emphasis on doctrine which relied on knowledge and thought. They called it "dead orthodoxy." Ironically, Kilian with his emphasis on the confessions was returning to orthodoxy, yet the conventicles which emerged from the pietistic movement supported him and used his materials to strengthen their faith. Kilian rejected the emotional

movements, but found some of their hymns such as "Es glänzet der Christen inwendiges Leben" and "O wie selig sind die Seelen," appealing. Kilian to G. A. Schierferdecker, 2 September 1869 (CHI); Kilian to Smoler, 15 June 1868 *Serbske Nowiny* 24 July 1869.

29. Nielsen, 66.

30. Korla A. Eckert, "Entstehung und Geschichte der evang.-Luth. Gemeinden Weigersdorf-Klitten," Mimeographed paper (T); Korla A. Eckert, "125-jähriges Kirchweihjubiläum der Evg.-Luth. Trinitatisgemeinde zu Weigersdorf OL," typed paper .

31. In a sermon given at the dedication of the church at Klitten, Kilian spelled out the conflict between the Calvinist teaching of the Lord's Supper which maintained that the bread and wine represented Christ's body and blood and the Lutheran view which held that the bread and wine were also Christ's body and blood. *Kirchenblatt für die Gemeinden evangelisch-lutherischen Bekenntnisses in der Preußischen Staaten*, January 1848 pp. 2-16; February 1848 pp. 24-32.

32. Malinkowa, 103.

33. Eckert.

34. Malinkowa, 104-105.

35. Kilian to Harless, 24 November 1851.

36. Malinkowa, 112; Hauptmann, 101.

37. Kilian to Colleague 22 February 1850 (W); Kilian to Colleague 18 October 1853 (W); Parish Report ca. 1849 - 1851 (W)

38. Malinkowa, 113-114; Parish Report ca. 1849-1851.

39. Kilian to Stempel, 1 July 1852 (W); Kilian to Pastor, 29 July 1852 (W).

40. Kilian to Colleague, 22 February 1850.

41. Kilian to Harless, 24 November 1851.

42. Malinkowa, 111.

43. *Tydzenske Nowiny* July, 1853, 240. *Kirchenblatt für die evang.-Lutherischen Gemeinen in Preußen*, 15 April 1854, p. 98,99; Johann Kasper letter, *Serbske Nowiny*, 18 March 1854; Malinkowa 119-120; In 1867 Kilian wrote that "the legalism of the Breslau church administration forced me to emigrate to America in 1854." Kilian to Lindemann, 11 April 1867. There was also a rub between Kilian and the Breslau group over money. Kilian to J. Greve, 7 September 1869, (TWHS).

44. The Saxon migration of 1838 that later supported the formation of the Missouri Synod also paid for the passage of people who could not afford it. Forester, 164-7.

45. God's Word and Luther's teaching pure, shall to eternity endure.

46. *Leipziger Zeitung*, 7 September 1854; Malinkowa, 120;

47. *Budissiner Nachrichten*, 4 January 1855.

48. *The New Handbook of Texas* (Austin: Texas State Historical Association, 1996), III, 1094; *Leipziger Zeitung*, 7 September 1854. In *Geschichte der Sorben*, a history written during communist control of East Germany and one that interpreted events in harmony with that ideology, Kilian was portrayed as a utopian who would solve the social and nationalistic problems of the Wends by taking all the Wends out

of Germany. 135. Yet another view, also assigning him a significant role in the leadership and often found in journalistic accounts, identifies him as a 19th century Moses, leading his people to the promised land.

49. Kilian to Andreas Dutschmann, 19 March 1855, *Serbske Nowiny* 9 June 1855.

50. The ship, an 80 foot long packet, was only two years old. *Budissiner Nachrichten*, 4 January 1855.

51. On the *Inconstant*, 9 October 1854 CHI.

52. Kilian to Walther, 9 February 1855; Seven more people died between Galveston and Rabbs Creek. Joseph Wilson, "Pastor Johann Kilian's Shipboard Diary," *Concordia Historical Quarterly*, 1985, 152. Joseph Wilson ed. "The August Haak Diary of the Wendish Emigration to Texas in 1854 on the Ben Nevis" *Journal of the German - Texas Heritage Society*, 13 (1991) 116-122; Johann Sommer to Parents (ca. 1855-1861) In author's possession.

53. Kilian to Clamour Schuermann, 11 June 1859, *Australischer Christenbote*, October and November 1860.

Chapter II – Kilian in Texas 1854-1884

1. Jack R. Wiederhold to author, 4 April 2001.

2. Kilian had been in relatively good health for most of his life although in 1873 he suffered a recurring illness with typhoid or "bilious" fever that lasted from July until December. The illness was severe enough to prevent him from preaching and for one period there were nine Sundays with someone reading the sermon. Kilian to J. F. Bünger, 25 November 1873 (CHI).

3. C. F. W. Walther to Kilian 9 February 1867 (CHI).

4. Kilian to father-in-law of Matthiez, 18 December 1857 (W); Kilian to Hermann Kilian, 20 November 1876 (TWHS); Kilian to Bünger, 25 November 1873. Kilian had written to President Bünger about Theresia in the hope that an educated male would inquire. When no one showed an interest, Kilian blamed the church division for discrediting him and in turn reducing chances for a suitable spouse.

5. Kilian to Bünger, 25 November 1873.

6. Kilian to O. Hanser, 12 December 1877 (TWHS).

7. Kilian to Hermann, 20 November 1876.

8. Wiederhold to the author, 4 April 2001; *Der Lutheraner*, 15 November 1884, 171-172; 1 December 1884, 180-181.

9. Kilian to Andreas Dutschmann, 19 March 1855, *Serbske Nowiny* 9 June 1855.

10. Kilian to Dutschmann, 19 March 1855. To avoid some freight costs Kilian stored the heavy books in Houston and also placed his wagon up for sale.

11. George R. Nielsen, *In Search of a Home: Nineteenth-Century Wendish Immigration* (College Station, Texas: Texas A & M University Press, 1989), 76, 77; Mrs. Helas to Friend, *Serbske Nowiny*, 24 March 1855; F. G. Seydler to editor, *Serbske Nowiny*, 7 July 1855; Kilian to Gotthold Gumlich, 20 December 1857 (W).

12. Kilian to Dutschmann 19 March 1855.

13. Johann Kasper Letter, 26 December 1853, *Serbske Nowiny*, 18 March 853.

14. Nielsen, 78.

15. Kilian to Congregation, 14 October 1855 (CHI); Kilian to father-in-law of Matthiez, 18 December 1857.

16. Kasper Letter, 26 December 1853; Kilian to Gumlich 20 December 1857; Call to Kilian, 25 March 1854 (CHI); Kilian to Congregation, 14 October 1855; Kilian to Walther, 25 June 1858 (CHI); Bastrop County Census 1860. In 1858 Kilian owned 19 head of cattle, 16 hogs, and 1 horse. Kilian to Gumlich 20 May 1858. Kilian's European opponents would criticize him for his property and implying that he neglected his ministry.

17. Breslau Oberkirchen Kollegium.

18. H. C. Ziehe, *A Centennial History of the Lutheran Church in Texas, 1851-1951* (Seguin, Texas, 1954), 40 - 42; Kilian to Bünger 21 October 1872 (CHI). Braun soon severed his connection with the Texas Synod and remained separate from any synodical ties until 1876 when he joined the Missouri Synod. However, three years later members of the congregation brought charges and he was dismissed from the Synod. When he refused to give up the congregation, the dissenting members withdrew and formed a Missouri Synod church, Trinity Lutheran. He died in 1880. W. H. Bewie, *Missouri in Texas: A History of the Lutheran Church - Missouri Synod in Texas 1855 - 1941* (Austin: The Texas District, 1952), 25, 26.

19. The official name of the Missouri Synod was Die Evangelische-lutherische Synode von Missouri, Ohio, und Andere Staaten. The word "synod" can be used to identify an assembly or an association of churches. It simply means "walking together" and the assumption is that there was a level of religious consensus among the participants. A synod, when used as an association of congregations, can also be subdivided into smaller units called districts. The elected head of the Missouri Synod as well as the elected head of each district is called "president." At the time of Kilian's migration Texas was part of the Western District. In 1882, shortly prior to his death, Texas was assigned to the newly created Southern District.

20. Kilian to Walther, 9 February 1855 (CHI). Walther refers to Kilian as "Studiengenosse" or fellow student. Walther joined the pietist circle as a theological student.

21. Kilian to Walther, 9 February 1855. Kilian to G. A. Schieferdecker 28 June 1869 (CHI).

22. Kilian to Walther; 9 February 1855; Most pastors benefit from collegiality because of the nature of their office that isolates them from the parishioners. The author's grandfather, Pastor E. F. Moerbe, during his ministry in Giddings at the turn of the century, was a frequent host to the rural pastors when they came to Giddings to shop. His daughter Esther remembered being given a tin bucket with a lid and sent to get it filled with beer while the pastors socialized, discussed theology, sermon texts, and problems of the parish.

23. Kilian to Saxon church 21 Dec. 1865 (CHI); Kilian to Lindemann, 11 April 1867 (CHI); "Good friends are like staffs…" Kilian to Lindemann, 8 May 1867 (CHI).

24. Kilian to Gumlich, 26 May 1858 (CHI); Kilian to Walther, 25 June, 1858. The division of the two groups was evident during the voyage when on the ship *Inconstant* the group elected a church council of five, three were from Prussia and two from Saxony. "On the *Inconstant*" 9 October 1854 (CHI). The conventicles in Saxony were widespread, and Kilian said, "I put up with these [conventicles] for 11 years in my ministry…in Saxony." Kilian specifically mentioned two: at Rakel and Cortnitz.

25. Kilian to Gumlich, 20 December 1857; Kilian to Gumlich, 26 May 1858; Kilian to Walther, 25 June 1858.

26. On the original document Jacob Urban penciled in behind his name: "I now have found a firm foundation." It is a line from the hymn sung to the melody "Oh that I had a thousand voices." Kilian copied the letter and signatures and sent it to Europe, but he did not copy Urban's comment. Dissidents to Kilian, 25 May 1858 (CHI).

27. Congregation to Dissidents, June, 1858 (CHI); Kilian to Gumlich, 19 October 1858 W; Arthur C. Repp, "St. Paul's and St. Peter's Lutheran Churches, Serbin, Texas, 1855 - 1905," *Concordia Historical Institute Quarterly*, January, 1943, 116.

28. Trudla Malinkowa, *Ufer der Hoffnung* (Bautzen, Germany: Domowina-Verlag, 2nd. edition, 1999), 149; Kilian to Lindemann, 11 April 1867; Kilian to Lindemann, 8 May 1867.

29. Kilian to Walther, 2 May 1867 (CHI); Kilian to Ebert, 11 March 1868 (CHI); Kilian to Walther 2 May 1867 (CHI).

30. English sermon, 1859, (CHI).

31. Even though Kilian's mission was not to the English speaking people, the church must have attracted curious people who were not versed in the proper Lutheran church decorum. Six years later, on April 8, 1866 instead of excluding the guests, the congregational meeting adopted the following rules and had them posted in the two Serbin stores and published in the Bastrop newspaper. 1. It is forbidden for men to wear hats during the worship. 2. It is not permissible to smoke a pipe or chew tobacco in the church building. 3. It is forbidden to carry six-shooters or any other weapon into the church. 4. It is not permissible for anyone to leave the church during the worship. 5. It is not permissible to enter or to leave the church in a noisily or disturbing manner. 6. It is not permissible to speak aloud in or near the church while services are being held. 7. It is not permissible to laugh in church. 8. It is not permissible to laugh as though in sport in front of the church windows or doors. *The Texas Messenger* February 6, 1972.

32. *Kirchenblatt für die evang.-Lutherischen Gemeinen in Preußen*, 1 Nov 1854, 265, 266.

33. Kilian to Gumlich, 19 October 1858; Kilian to Gumlich, 16 December 1858; At other times Kilian requested that some things would not be published because he knew the Missouri Synod leadership subscribed to the journal and might

read it. Kilian closed the letter: "I remain your devoted cattle-breeder and farmer." Evidently the European opponents charged that Kilian was neglecting the ministry and devoting too much time to his property.

34. Kilian Letter 18 December 1857; Kilian to Gumlich 23 March 1859; Kilian to Gumlich 6 July 1859.

35. Jan Korla Lehmann to Jan Smoler, 10 December 1859, *Serbske Nowiny* 4 February 1860; Kilian to Smoler, 15 June 1868 *Serbske Nowiny* 24 July 1869; Kilian to Smoler, 12 December 1872 (CHI).

36. Kilian to Smoler, 22 August 1872 (CHI); *Lausitzisch wendisches Wörterbuch* (Budissin, 1866) In the preface Pfuhl credits Kilian with a "small collection of words." He is probably referring to the list of words in the Sorb archives rather than the list prepared in Texas.

37. Kilian's most critical comments toward the Germans were made in his letter to Bünger on November 2, 1869 (TWHS). "The German nationality since Adam's fall possessed the tendency to enslave."

38. Anne Blasig, *The Wends of Texas* (San Antonio: The Naylor Company, 1954), 61; Malinkowa 151; Kilian to Lindemann, 11 April 1867.

39. Kilian to Brohm, 21 April 1870 (CHI); Kilian to Walther, 4 April 1870 (CHI); Kilian to J. Greve, 7 September 1869 (TWHS); Kilian could not understand how people so filled with hate could attend communion together. Kilian to Bünger, 9 December 1869 (CHI). Congregational Minutes 22 May 1870, 12 June 1870 (CHI); Joseph Wilson (ed. and trans.), *Pastor Johann Kilian's Baptismal Records of St. Paul Lutheran Church, Serbin, Texas 1854 – 1883* (Serbin, Texas: St. Paul Lutheran Church, 1985). Because both congregations belonged to the same synod, members could change their membership only through transfer. This procedure was to be initiated by a member by requesting the voters to grant a release from the congregation. After Pallmer's death, St. Peter's congregation dropped the Wendish services and some Wendish families who hoped to transfer back to St. Paul's experienced difficulty obtaining the release. Similar tensions became evident when a member of one congregation married a person from the other.

40. Kilian, when mentioning the distance to Fedor, always said it was 12 miles away. He also referred to the people of Fedor as his tormentors who moved to the Yegua Creek and became Pastor Proft's tormentors. Kilian to Hermann, 5 November 1874 (TWHS).

41. Kilian to Walther, 7 March 1871 (CHI); Kilian to Bünger, 7 August 1873 (CHI); Kilian to K. A. Mattig, 23 August 1872 (CHI).

42. Kilian to Caspar Braun, 4 October 1870 (TWHS); Kilian to Bünger, 7 August 1873; Kilian to Petr Brojer, 18 June 1874 (CHI); Kilian to Herman, 28 February 1876 TWHS; Kilian to Johann Zimmermann, 3 September 1873 (TWHS); Kilian to Bünger, 25 November 1873. Pastor Geyer, Walther's cousin and part of the Saxon migration, was an orthodox theologian and an experienced pastor. One can readily infer that the choice by the church officials was a deliberate one made in the hope of stabilizing the relations between the two Serbin parishes.

43. Lehmann to Smoler, 8 March 1870, *Serbske Nowiny* 16 April 1870; Arthur C. Repp, "St. Paul's and St. Peter's Lutheran Churches, Serbin, Texas 1855-1905"

Concordia Historical Institute Quarterly (April, 1944) p. 28. The registers of the congregation are held at St. Paul church.

44. Kilian to Gumlich, 20 December 1857; Kilian Letter 16 January 1857 (CHI); Kilian to Gumlich, 20 May 1858.

45. John B. Koch, *When the Murray Meets the Mississippi: A Survey of Australian and Lutheran Contacts, 1838 – 1934* (Adelaide: Lutheran Publishing House, 1975), 80. Koch credits Kilian for much of the growth of Australian–American Lutheran relations, 31; Kilian felt Walther's coolness and commented, "I once hoped that I had found a friend in Professor Walther, but he seems to draw back, probably because he is the President and because he has some doubts about me. He is friendly as always but reserved." Kilian to Lindemann, 11 April 1867. Walter R. Rast Jr. in "Pietism and Mission: Lutheran Millennialism in the Eighteenth and Nineteenth Centuries" *Concordia Theological Quarterly* (October 2000), 295-317 argues for the compatibility of pietism and millennialism. Kilian opposed pietism demonstrated in the conventicles yet supported millennialism.

46. Kilian to Bautzen clergyman, *Serbske Nowiny*, 1866, No. 6, 43-44; Kilian to Rudolph Rychtar, 3 November 1874, Sorbisches Kulturarchiv.

47. Malinkowa, 158; Kilian to Rudolph Richter, 30 January 1873 (CHI); Kilian to Walther, February 1873 (CHI); Kilian to Max Frommel, 2 November 1873 (CHI); Kilian to Frommel, 9 March 1874 (CHI); Kilian to Frommel, May, 1877 (CHI); Kilian to Gottfried Fritschel, 26 January 1880, Wartburg Seminary, Dubuque, Iowa.

48. In 1883, a year before his death, Kilian did indeed construct a Wendish *Agenda* or order of service. Possibly his son's assumption of the congregational responsibilities freed him for the task. It was not printed until 1909 and was never bound and sold. Daphne Dalton Garrett, *Giddings Deutsches Volksblatt, 1899-1949: A History of the Newspaper and Print Shop of the Texas Wends* (Warda, Texas: D. D. Garrett, 1998).

49. Kilian to Dutschmann 19 March 1855, *Serbske Nowiny* 9 June 1855; Kilian to Gumlich, 20 December 1857; Kilian to Gumlich 16 December 1858; Kilian to Gumlich, 20 May 1858.

50. Lehmann to Smoler, 10 December 1859, *Serbske Nowiny* 4 February 1860; Kilian to Kirchenrath, 16 June 1864 (CHI).

51. Kilian to Lindemann, 11 April 1867; Kilian to Lindemann, 8 May 1867; Kilian to Schieferdecker, 28 June 1869 (CHI).

52. Kilian to Smoler, 15 June 1868 *Serbske Nowiny* 24 July 1869.

53. Malinkowa, 159; Kilian to Brojer, 18 June 1874; Kilian to Bünger, 22 January 1874 (CHI); Kilian to Hermann, 28 February 1876 (TWHS); Kilian to Mattig, 23 August 1872; Kilian to Braun, 5 February 1874 (CHI).

54. Kilian to Wjelan, *Serbske Nowiny* 27 February 1879, pp. 247-8.

55. Kilian to Richter, 30 January 1873; Malinkowa 160.

INDEX